Acknowledgements

Tammy "Nahlah" Butler — As-Salaam wa-laikum, wa-Rahmatullah, wa-Barakatuhuh. Thank you for your confidence and your tremendous amount of support and help. You have grown into a truly dynamic person, word up. You have put a lot of things into play; handling both A&R duties, as well as Project Coordination. And with every new endeavor you have improved. Project cleared, nahmean… Smash City Crew: "Stacky Mack" (H. Stax) — What the deal, son, WHENVER I needed somethin', you ALWAYS held me down: Real is Real, word up. Rone (Mike Rone) — Real is Real, you among the small number of dependable people that I know; Boog (B) — Real is Real, yo, son, we get down, yo spot is reserved, nahmean; Eon (E) — Real is Real, you understand the process, so like I said, be ready, feel me… Cus — Yo, fam', what I tell you! You know we gotta' do now. Thank you for makin' sure that I make my recording sessions on time. (Your new Camry is on its way)… Marlo Printing: Yo, Jay (Jayson), man listen, my heaviest gratitude. Because of your professionalism, generosity and friendship, I was easily able to manufacture and distribute the first two editions of BeatTips™. You are one of the realest that I know. Thank you. Leo, good-lookin' out. Thanks for helping me with everything from printing to the basics of various software programs. And as with Jay, thanks for makin' it more than just business, nahmean… Joanne Nathan (Co-Owner/Manager- Unique Recording Studios) — Thank you Joanne for recognizing my company as a contender. Thank you for my rates and thank you for the recommendation and reference that you provided. You are a very kind person… Maxine Simpson   Sincere, understanding and professional, thank you for keeping our business personal! Marsh (Marsha) right there, right on time, and always straight up with it… Abigal ("Abbie") — You came through in the 11th hour — one of the best examples of makin' the most of an opportunity!

Finally, I would like to extend my respect and gratitude to Hip Hop-Rap's Elite Pioneers: Marley Marl, DJ Premier, Large Professor, DJ Pete Rock, and The RZA. Their numerous developments, discoveries and overall contributions can never be ignored.

BeatTips™ Manual

Some Insight on Producing Hip Hop-Rap Beats and Music

Third Edition

Written and Created

by

SA'ID

Published by

SUPERCHAMP
Books™

BeatTips Manual: Some Insight on Producing
Hip Hop-Rap Beats and Music.
by Sa'id
1. Author 2. Title 3. Music 4. Hip Hop-Rap Producing 5. Vocational Training

Library of Congress Control Number 2004093131
ISBN 0-9749704-3-3 (Paperback)

Proofread by Qamar
Typeset by Sharon for Docufit™

Edited by Sa'id

Design and Layout by Sa'id
Cover design by Sa'id

Praise be to Allah, the Almighty, who by His infinite Mercy enabled me to write this book. Any faults in this book are mine, any good in this book is from Allah.

Al-Humdullilah Ar-Rahmanir Rahim
(All Praise and Thanks is for Allah, the Most Gracious, the Most Merciful).

QAMAR and AMIR... As-Salaam wa-laikum, wa-Rahmatullah, wa-Barakatuhuh.
Your support, patience and most importantly, your advice, was extremely helpful – and that's by default! AMIR you handle way more responsibilities than many people four and five times your age, without any complaints and in a very creatively professional manner. I thank Allah for you and your understanding, and your accurate insight...

SANDRA (my mother) One of the best things that you ever did: *buying me that typewriter when I was a kid*! Though things may have been kind of hard for us, I thank you for sacrificin' and tryin' to make my life a little easier. May Allah guide you.

All praise is for Allah, we praise Him, and we seek His help and His forgiveness. We seek refuge with Allah from the evil of ourselves and our deeds. Whomsoever Allah guides, no one can mislead him; and whomsoever He leads astray, none can guide him.

I bear witness that none has the right to be worshipped but Allah, alone, without any partners and I bear witness that Muhammad is His servant and Messenger.

Contents

Introduction

MAKING HIP HOP-RAP BEATS and Music is an easily accessible craft, but a difficult one to master. Anyone can buy electronic instruments and pro audio equipment. However, the purchase of equipment does not guarantee that anyone will develop a unique skill for music production. The fact is, most people who venture into the Hip Hop-Rap music production field fail to ever earn a living from their production services! Now, I've known a number of Producers, who were quick to point out that they didn't measure success by "payments and paychecks"…that it's "all about the love and passion for the music." I partially agree with this sentiment. On one hand, I do believe that a producer should enjoy producing, or at least like it. On the other hand, I respect the fact that "success" is relative to each producer, I think that success is determined by the development of a producer's own unique style and sound, as well as some financial compensation for that Producer's services.

Creating music for the purpose of sharing it with family, friends and co-workers is any producer's prerogative. More power to them! However, one of the main goals of my manual is to encourage producers to develop their skill, with the ultimate goal of self employment and self reliance. I strongly feel that the best way to earn a decent living is by incorporating your own individual talents and skills. The overwhelming majority of workers, in any profession throughout the world, often dislike or even hate their jobs and careers. But Hip Hop-Rap Music Producers, especially those who take pride in their personal development, are unique because they have the opportunity to earn a living, by simply doing something they enjoy. With this theme in mind, I designed BeatTips™ to help producers develop and increase their production skills, while at the same time offer insight on how they can best manifest their production expertise into a successful career.

There are a number of reasons that contribute to the success or failure of Hip Hop-Rap music Producers. Indeed, only a small number will ultimately be successful. In my opinion, the success of a Hip Hop-Rap music producer depends first and foremost on the development of their own unique sound and style. For a Producer to create and develop their own unique sound and style, there are many factors that must be "honestly" considered. For instance: What kind of person are you? Are you very organized and disciplined? Or are you disorganized, and often undisciplined? Do you have a vast musical knowledge that spans over multiple musical genres? Do you use classic or contemporary

Notes

electronic instruments and pro-audio equipment? Do you prefer using Hardware Samplers or Keyboards? Do you like sampling records or do you prefer live instrumentation? All of these questions address some of the most critical aspects of making Hip Hop-Rap Beats and Music. Hence, the primary aim of BeatTips™ is to help Hip Hop-Rap Music Producers identify and manipulate the various aspects that are critical to creating and developing their own unique Production sounds and styles.

The BeatTips™ Manual covers the whole process of making Hip Hop-Rap Beats and Music. From **Getting Gear** to **Sampling**; from **Drum Programming** to **Sequencing**; from **Building a Beat & Music Catalogue** to **Shopping and Selling Your Beats and Music**… This manual explores these areas and many more, in a very simple, easy-to-read fashion. Every section is clear and concise. In fact, the entire manual is easy to navigate. Throughout each section, I've included the header: **BeatTip™**. This header should be viewed as a special alert. Whenever you see the BeatTip™, pay very close attention or you might miss a very important tip! Also, I have made the table of contents descriptive enough to allow skipping ahead. Though I do not recommend skimming ahead on your first read, you can still aggressively find what you need, by simply checking the proper heading on the table of contents page. For example, if you're interested in bass filtering, you can go directly to the section and look for the heading that reads: Filtering: Bass. You may also check the index for the topic you want help on. Here, you'll find page numbers for where this topic is discussed.

Finally, I should point out that I use a classic setup production setup: an Akai S950 MIDI Digital Sampler and an Akai MPC 60II (Midi Production Center). I discuss method and technique in reference to this setup and these units first and foremost! However, in universal areas, such as Sampling, I didn't restrict technique and method references to my setup, or any particular gear, for that matter. But, I must point out that the setup that I use produces a number of sound and technical effects that are unique to this particular gear combination, only. Understand, no two Digital Samplers or Drum Machines and/or Sequencers are the exact same. They all process and convert MIDI signals in the manner in which each were designed. Different electronic instruments and equipment combine to produce various effects. What one Producer may be able to do on a particular setup, another Producer may not be able to do on yet another setup! Where one Producer is limited by a particular setup, another Producer may find numerous possibilities. In regards to equipment and gear, and setups in general, the tips that I offer cover both the **fundamental** *and* **advanced principles** of

Notes

making Hip Hop-Rap Beats and Music. And even though most of the technique, Sample Editing and Sequencing tips that I offer are specifically inspired and related to an Akai S950/Akai MPC 60II setup, a good number of tips that I offer can and should be applied to all gear and pro audio equipment, and all production setups in general.

Notes

Getting Your Gear

BEFORE YOU GET A SINGLE piece of gear or equipment, I suggest that you first identify the kinds and types of beats and music that you wanna' make. Of all the producers and rappers that you listen to and like, you probably already have a "core" of favorites… For whatever reason: you like the smooth sound of this one Producer. Or you like how this other Producer has a raw, rough sound… Or you like how yet another Producer features instrumentation in his production… Or you like how yet another Producer "flips" his samples… ALL OF THIS IS VALID.

The sounds and styles that you hear from the Producers you admire are the results of **A LOT OF PRACTICE** and other tangibles, including: their base region and environment, their musical tastes, their core market (audience), etc. **Likewise, the gear that each Producer uses is not only a highly personal choice, it is a major part of their overall style and technique.** The equation goes like this:

Producer, plus Gear, dictates sound ™

No two producers are the same. Some producers practice much more than others. Some producers have more desire and discipline. Some producers listen to and study lots of music, and therefore, take on a variety of recording projects. So, "who" you are as a person/producer is the most significant part in the equation of making beats and music. The only other part in the equation is the gear that you use…

Check this out:

Before I got my first pieces of equipment, which consisted of a hand-me-down, belt-drive Technics turntable, a Panasonic direct-drive turntable, an old metal-plated Numark DJ mixer, a pioneer stereo receiver and a pair of CBX speakers, I didn't *really* know what a producer was. I wanted to be a DJ! My idea of a producer was Quincy Jones. When I was a little kid, I remember seeing his name on an old **Brothers Johnson** album. As I grew older, I saw his name on variety of albums, including the score and soundtrack for the movie, *The Wiz*. So, I associated the term "Music Producer" with someone like Quincy Jones. Even though DJ'ing remained cool, writing was what I had began doing, before anything… (I mostly wrote short stories and poems). **"So, when Hip Hop was originated"**, I gravitated into writing rhymes.

Notes

I didn't really get serious about writin' rhymes until I was 18 or 19. I soon learned that *everybody* was writin' rhymes! This meant that you had to wait for beats. I didn't really know anyone who was producing beats. After I finally hooked up with this one producer up in Harlem, it became even harder to get beats. He was making beats for M.C.s from all over New York: Harlem, the Bronx, Brooklyn, Queens… all at the same time. Every now and then, when it wasn't too many cats in the studio, he would let me mess'around with his equipment, which included an E-MU SP1200 Drum Machine/Sampler/Sequencer and an Akai S900 Digital Sampler setup. Unfortunately, he never taught me anything. He would always say: "it's too complex to get into, right now." Yo, for real, at that time, I was impressed just by those red and green digital meter lights, that went up and down on the mixing board. So, I believed that it was complex… Anyway, one day this other M.C. and I wanted to claim this particular beat. You know what the only solution was: we had to battle for it! It was ruled a draw, and the producer gave us both "cassette" copies of the beat that same day.

"Battlin' for a beat was real, but I didn't write battle rhymes. And when I thought about it, this producer's beats didn't really inspire or fit what I was trying to do, vocally or musically. So, that day I knew I had to get my own equipment…"

My first major production equipment was an E-Mu SP1200 Sampling Drum Machine/Sequencer and an Akai S01 Digital Sampler. I actually wanted to get an Akai S900, but I couldn't afford it (or so I thought at the time). And even if I could, I didn't know where to get a *brand new one.*

Also, I didn't know what a **Basic Gear Setup**[1] was, and I didn't know about the used gear business at all. I asked that same producer—the only producer I knew personally at the time—which equipment did he recommend

---

[1]**Basic Gear Setup** — To produce Hip Hop-Rap beats and music you need a basic set of equipment and gear. Producers are very subjective about this, however the basics include: 1. A device that creates or samples drum sounds, either a Drum Machine or a Sampling Drum Machine or Keyboard; 2. A device that samples sounds and other music, like a Digital Sampler or a Sound Module or a Keyboard with sampling capabilities; 3. A device that sequences your equipment, like a Sampling Drum Machine with a Sequencer, a Keyboard or a Midi Keyboard Controller; 4. A Turntable; 5. Something that allows you to hear audio, like Studio Monitors or Speakers (I use speakers); and 6. A CD Recorder or Cassette Deck, something to record your music to. Depending on your budget and needs, you could opt for a Multitrack Recorder, which in plain talk, is basically a combination of a mixing console and a Digital CD Recorder. Another recording option and sequencing option could be a software program, such as Pro Tools. However, YOU DO NOT NEED Pro tools to record your music, as some producers may wrongfully assert; 7. A Power Source, an Amplifier.

Notes

that I get and where should I go to get it. He told me to go to Sam Ash. He said: "they'll have everything that you need." I went to Sam Ash, they didn't have an Akai S900. However they did have the SP1200... and the salesman convinced me that I wouldn't be giving up too much if I went with the Akai S01. If you know what an Akai S01 is, you know exactly how much you're giving up! As it turned out, I gave up critical gear capability, particularly the ability to filter out sounds. (For more on filtering, see the Filtering section, beginning on pg. 24)

I didn't know **Gear-Capability™²**and what that meant to me. I thought, "If it samples, then everything else should be cool." Everything else was not cool. There were a lot of things that I wanted to do musically, but because I couldn't do them on that Akai S01, I actually believed that they couldn't be done at all.

"There were so many sounds I didn't sample, simply because I thought that the "highs" and "lows" couldn't be manipulated!"

What I didn't know, for instance, was that some digital samplers (like the Akai S900 that I originally wanted), came with **filters.** I didn't even know what a filter was! But when I was in Sam Ash that day, I assumed that I was buying a better sampler. I incorrectly thought that, since the Akai S01 was a newer model, it *had* to have everything that the S900 featured and more... Try and you learn, right! Unfortunately, over the next several years, I continued to make this sort of a mistake. I went through a lot of very expensive and completely unnecessary gear and equipment changes. And the result was that my production development suffered tremendously.

BeatTip™

Honestly decide which producer(s) you really like. You probably have three to five favorites, but choose the one's who's music that you feel the most. Consider if these producers feature Sampling in their production. Studying

---

My recommended Basic Gear Set-Up includes: an Akai S950 Digital Sampler, with the memory fully expanded; an Akai MPC 60II (a sampling drum machine with sequencer); a Technics SL-1200 MK2 Turntable; a Mackie 1604 VLZ 16 channel mixing board; a HHB CDR 850 CD Recorder; Speakers with a lot of bass; a Hafler P3000 Amplifier; and a Sure SM58 Microphone, with a line input adapter. This setup will train you thoroughly, while at the same time, should you need to add to this setup it will prompt you. That is, this setup, though Classic (vintage) in nature, is actually still VERY relevant to contemporary Hip Hop-Rap Music. Therefore, as you develop, you may find that the ONLY additions *actually necessary* may simply be a late model Keyboard/Synth or Sound Module.
² **Gear-Capability** — The functions, features and potential of a particular piece of gear or equipment.

Notes

producers that like to use live instrumentation instead of samples won't hurt you. But you'll be hard pressed to match or surpass their sound, if you do not favor live instrumentation. At first, you should mainly study the producers that make the kind of beats and music that you want to make, using the kinds of methods (i.e. record samples), that you envision yourself using.

The idea is to **NEVER COPY** another producer's sound or style. But the reality is, in every artistic or creative format, techniques, styles, etc. will undoubtedly be "mirrored", and in some cases, out-right stolen. The art of Hip Hop-Rap Music Production is no different in this aspect. Every producer has "taken" a piece of some other producer's sound, attack, style and/or technique. Remember the late 80s/early 90s? One producer began sampling James Brown records, then nearly every producer began doing the same. Point is, the better producers know how to incorporate the new "tips" that they get into there own production! So, there is absolutely nothing wrong with taking your initial lead from the producers that you admire. Remember, every great artist, or producer (even the modern pioneers) in ANY musical genre, got their lead from someone. In regards to Hip Hop-Rap Music, it's common knowledge who the earliest production pioneers were: Marley Marl, DJ Premier, The Large Professor, DJ Pete Rock, and The RZA, to name some of the main ones. (see the **Producers and/or Recording Artists of Special Note** section for a broader list). So, in some form or fashion, every producer and/or pioneer that came after these early production pioneers, gained from their lead.

O.K., now, after you key in on the producers that you really admire, you have to find out what gear and pro audio equipment that they use. If you do not already know, there's one cool way to do this. It involves a lot of research on your part, but in the end, the rewards are much bigger. The first thing that you do is read the credits for a project that you know for certain that they produced. Locate the name of the recording studio in which they recorded the particular production project that you're interested in. Get the number to that recording studio, then call and ask to speak with the Studio Manager. Open the conversation (with the Studio Manager) by explaining that you are considering recording your entire album project at their studio. Then inquire about the gear that they have, particularly, what samplers, keyboards, etc., that they have. After you've got the Studio Manager talking gear, ask them if they recall what gear "so-n-so" producer used the last time they were there. If they know off-hand, they'll tell you. But usually, they'll contact the engineer or assistant engineer who actually worked the session. If at all possible, you should want to speak to that engineer, directly. This way, you'll not only learn exactly which gear and equipment the producer of interest uses, you'll get some more tangible information.

Notes

Most engineers know gear and pro audio equipment. But more importantly, they often know **Gear-Capability™**. So, when you speak to an engineer, ask them what gear do they recommend for making Hip Hop-Rap beats and music. It's a very broad question, some would even say, it's a dumb question. But remember, broad questions usually get broad answers. If you don't know much about gear, like I didn't, you will want to get as much information as possible. So don't worry about sounding stupid. It's stupid not to ask questions or get any tips from those who know gear and production.

Check this out:

I once asked an engineer: **"Why do you need a mixing board?"** After he paused on the phone, he explained to me that a mixing board allows you to isolate and "mix" individual tracks and channels. He went on to explain how and *why* a mixing board is absolutely critical to the entire recording process. Then he asked me when was I considering coming in for a session. After that, he offered to engineer my session *at a discounted rate*. Man listen, I booked a session while we were still on the phone. (Mind you, at the time I didn't have any money…) I spent the next 8 days raising money, not for gear, but for this session. I used the money that I had actually been saving up to buy new equipment and gear with and I borrowed the rest from some family and friends.

On the night of the session, I rented the equipment that "I heard" a certain producer had used, and I brought in "dummy" floppy disks. Basically, what this means is, I brought in disks that I knew were blank, along with a few records that I had. I asked the assistant engineer if he could load up the disks—because I didn't know how. The engineer came over after the assistant engineer couldn't get the "dummy" disks loaded (wonder why). He told me that my disks were bad, and he asked me if I had brought back-ups with me. (Of course I didn't) so, I told him I had a few new ideas. I then proceeded to use the studio's turntable, and we (actually, more like he) sampled some sounds from the records I had brought with me to the session.

Throughout that very pivotal recording session, I was introduced to the basics of Digital Samplers, Drum Machines, and Sequencers. I learned, for instance, a little bit about what each machine was designed to do and how those designs could be manipulated. By the end of the session, I had a whole list of gear, complete with price estimates, that was a page long! So, from then on, determining what gear and pro audio equipment to get became a little easier. Armed with a list of equipment, I was ready. However, I still didn't know which equipment was right for me.

Notes

_____

_____

_____

_____

_____

_____

_____

_____

_____

_____

_____

_____

_____

_____

"Actually, it took me nearly FIVE YEARS before I finally found the right production setup. Had I known just 10% of what I know now about gear, its capabilities, and its best uses..."

BeatTip™

In addition to finding out which equipment your favorite producers use, the best way to determine which gear is right for you is to first determine what kinds of beats and music you wanna' make. Do you wanna' make club/party music? Do you wanna' make that old, basement style of Hip Hop-Rap. Do you wanna' make a combination of both? The sooner you *honestly* decide, the better off you'll be.

Obviously, all gear is not the same. However, certain kinds of gear clearly compliment certain kinds of beats and music. For example, the E-Mu SP 1200 is known for its raw, rough sound. But it is not a very warm-sounding unit (mainly because the frequency response level is too low). On the other hand, the Akai MPC 60II, which was designed to compliment the Akai S950, does sound warm. Of course, all production equipment can be manipulated in ways that can produce reverse effects. But keep in mind, this might mean going against the *nature* of the unit's overall design. Think of it as driving in reverse, up a one-way street: you can do it, but imagine how much harder you'll have to work, just to reach the end of the block... you're driving against the car's natural design.

Once you've determined what kind of sound that you wanna' make, and which electronic instruments will compliment that sound, you're ready to actually get your gear.

In the last 5 or so years, producers have become as recognizable (in some cases more) as recording artists, themselves. The makers and manufacturers of professional electronic instruments and pro audio equipment, who were in the dark at first, began focusing on Hip Hop-Rap and the rise of new producers, in the late 90s. Indeed, the development of Sampling technology and Sound Reproduction technology, most noticeably manifested in the creation of the Akai MPC 2000, has prompted a countless number of new machines, each OVERLY capable of performing such basic tasks as: Sampling, Sample Editing, Filtering, Looping, etc. On the real, for what I do, electronic instruments reached their peak between the late 80s and early 90s. My production style doesn't really require any inclusion of this newer technology. It's not that I completely reject any new Samplers or Drum Machines, or new technology for that matter. It's

Notes

just that, for what I do, I don't really *need* the newer technology.[3] The new electronic instruments, and we're basically talking Drum Machines, Digital Samplers, Sound Modules, Keyboards and Sequencers, offer a lot of "extra everything". They have "cleaner", "brighter" filters[4] with higher frequencies... More memory, more digital recording capabilities, just more, overall!

But "new" and "more" capabilities doesn't necessarily mean better. The newest equipment, loaded with new or more features, doesn't guarantee you a superior production level...

Used Gear

Considering the above, I suggest that you always begin your gear search on the Used Gear circuit. The Used Gear business has always thrived in the face of booming technological advancement. Like cars, used and out-dated musical gear will always sell! The fact is, the average person's economic situation can't keep pace with technology. So, what happens to the "out-dated" models of gear and equipment? Well, like cars, they still have value, even though they've been used. Hence, most "out-dated" or classic electronic instruments, gear and equipment are sold almost exclusively in Used Gear & Music Instrument Shops and on the internet.

BeatTip™

Clear an area in your home and firmly reserve that space as your future production area. Sitting somewhere within that reserved space, write a list of all the recording equipment and gear that you are interested in getting. Write down every piece that you are interested in getting. Don't worry about the cost at this point. The idea is to get a clear idea on what you want vs. what you actually need. After you've gotten your final list together, go hunting! I mean really look for it. Check out the Classifieds in your local newspapers, as well as major market areas like New York City and L.A. (The Village Voice, a newspaper published in NYC, has an excellent section for Used Musical Gear, Equipment and

---

[3] There are some cases where I have certainly benefited from some of the newer technology. In fact, some of the new technological developments are very useful, and outright practical! For instance, some times when I track music in larger, more equipped studios, I take full advantage of the editing features of Pro Tools!

[4] Devices within electronic instruments that enhance or remove high and low frequencies of a sound. For example, you could use filters to "take out" the high of a guitar part, thereby making it sound like a bass line.

Notes

Instruments. I suggest either getting a copy every week or simply going to their website at: www.villagevoice.com). Also, avoid a "simple-look". That is, don't just search for gear and equipment in those huge music chain stores.

"Start your search for the equipment and gear that you want in Used Musical Gear and Equipment Outlets, like online Gear Stores, and well-known Used Gear Shops."

If you are not familiar with online auctions, get familiarized immediately. Gear and equipment manufacturers are designing and releasing new models at a ridiculously rapid pace! Therefore, more and more gear is being labeled "vintage". Music stores are aware of this, but more importantly, people (in particular, producers) are VERY keen to this fact. Especially those who have been discouraged by the process of production. Those who just want to sell and get back as much money for their gear and equipment as possible. When you factor in the fact that new producers are developing and entering into the scene, at a rate that rivals the manufacturers' upgrades, plus throw in the fact that more and more people are becoming "web shoppers", it will not be long before "vintage" gear prices rise!

Ebay (www.ebay.com) is an excellent source for used and/or new gear and equipment. Often on eBay, you'll be able to get gear at prices well below what they sell for in Used Gear Music Shops and Online Music Stores! However, there is some minor risk involved when buying gear on eBay. I once bid on and won an Akai S950 Digital Sampler from this one particular eBay seller. After 7 months, I still haven't received the unit or a refund. To avoid this type of situation with eBay sellers or ANY online stores that specialize in used gear and equipment, do a thorough background check of the seller. ALWAYS get a legitimate telephone number. If the seller or online store doesn't have a legitimate telephone number, or worst yet, they refrain from giving it to you when you request it, do not do business with them. But to be fair, I've bought A LOT of gear off of eBay and from online gear and equipment stores. The overwhelming majority of transactions that I've had on eBay and other online gear and equipment sites were very smooth. So, I still endorse shopping for gear online, provided you've done a check on the seller and you're satisfied with the return policy.

Local and National (U.S.) newspapers are another excellent source for finding used gear & equipment. Go to the Classified section and scan *everything* about music. You'll be surprised who's selling what and for how little! Check for office liquidations, recording studio liquidations. Even look under music job opportunities.

Notes

_____

_____

_____

_____

_____

_____

_____

_____

_____

_____

_____

_____

_____

_____

Now, after, and only after, you've exhausted all of the used gear and equipment resources, check out the giant music store chains, like Sam Ash, Musician's Friend, Guitar Center, etc. These stores are usually good when it comes to obtaining and purchasing non-discontinued gear. And they are especially good for the purchase of *high-end* or VERY expensive gear and equipment. For example, I'd get a new mixing console at Sam Ash, simply because of the price protection guarantee and warranty. Sam Ash is really good with price matching. If you've seen a price for the gear that you want anywhere else, they'll usually match it; in most cases they'll even beat it. (This is not a paid endorsement of Sam Ash. It's just my experience with dealing with them). Another reason to actually shop at the giant music stores is, to create a connection at the store. Once you've established a connection or a contact at one of these stores, you'll be informed about special stock-clearance, "as-is", and Floor-Model sales. You'll also receive all sorts of discounts on equipment and gear and accessories, as you do more business with them.

O.K., now that you've researched the gear, and you've got a good idea of what's right for you and where to get it, here's how you get the gear with little or no money up front.

Most producers get equipment as they go along, or rather, as they can afford it. So don't worry too much about the total monetary sum, whenever you choose to buy gear. But if you're really impatient and you don't have the money, there's one way that you can raise money in a relatively quick fashion. If you have a lot a family and friends and you're well respected, you basically already have the money!

Everybody's borrowed money for something, at some point. Most of the time it's for nothing very meaningful. You know, like, $100 here and there to get through the week; maybe pay a bill, that sort of thing. Well, obtaining production gear and equipment is not only meaningful, it's an excellent investment, so why not borrow… It's commonly known that many successful entrepreneurs regularly borrow from their family and friends, in order to create and invest in businesses and other financial opportunities. Let's say you have solid relationships with ten family members and close friends. If you were able to borrow just $300 from each of them, you'd have $3000… That's enough for a really nice, complete production setup! Still, to many people, $300 is a lot of money. So, the amount that you borrow should actually be lower. And instead of ten people you can count on, why not try 20, or 30!

Notes

Here's what you do. Use what I call a **CBT™ (Creative Borrowing Technique™)**. It works like this. Make a list of 30 people you're pretty sure you can count on for $100 each. $100 is a very typical and reasonable sum of money to borrow, among close family and trusted friends and/or co-workers. More importantly, it's also relatively easy to pay back, especially if you structure it right. After you're satisfied with your list, devise a graduated repayment plan. Listen, before you even approach anyone about borrowing money, make sure that you can realistically fulfill your repayment plan. A good graduated repayment plan works like this: for every group of three people that you borrow $100 from, you agree to repay them back four weeks after the next group. For example, when you ask for a loan from a family member or friend, schedule your repayment in one month increments. Group 1 gets paid back in a month. Group 2 gets paid back in two months, and so on until everyone is paid back. Be up front with the people that you're borrowing from. If you can not pay them back for two or three months, let them know up front, as a part of the condition of the loan. Remember, you're asking people that respect you and your word for a small loan. So, as long as you can guarantee repayment within three months, you'll receive the loan. Just Make sure you give clear and very advanced notice as to when you'll need the money. Although everyone will be repaid on a different schedule, make sure that you secure all loans within the same time frame, let's say, like the same week. I've raised and repaid thousands of dollars using this very method. It's one of the fastest ways to obtain gear, with little or no money down. I actually financed the recording, manufacturing, promotion and distribution of my first album using this method.

Payment Plans

If borrowing money isn't your thing, and you only have a little cash, then get your gear piece by piece, as you can afford it. Most used musical instrument shops are understanding. 90% of the time they'll work with your situation. For instance, let's say you wanna' get an Akai MPC 60II and you've seen one listed at a used gear shop for $999. If you can put down at least $100 and agree to have it paid off within a month, it's usually a done deal. I've put down as little as $50 on equipment that was selling for over $1500. But I was diligent. Every five days, I somehow managed to put down at least an additional $100. I also called this particular shop at least a once week. The final result, after two months— and keep in mind, I really was supposed to have only one—was that I paid off the balance… The shop owner even gave me a 15% cash discount at the end of the sell. To this day, we're friends and we still do business.

Notes

_____

_____

_____

_____

_____

_____

_____

_____

_____

_____

_____

_____

_____

Tech Swaps

Do you have any computer equipment or home electronic equipment that you really do not need? I've gone to pawnshops many a times. I traded my T.V. before…I swapped a used Sharp 20" color television set for a drum machine and a Gemini Scratchmaster DJ Mixer. I also traded this Epson color printer I use to own, plus a VCR and a Nikon camera for a used E-Mu SP1200 Sampling Drum Machine/Sequencer. So, before you say you don't have the resources to get gear, look around your home and see what you can give up. Swapping your tech and home electronic equipment is a very viable way to obtain gear.

Barter

Most producers that I know have multiple skills that are somehow related to music and/or production. Graphic design, for instance, is a great skill to obtain. I bartered, or rather, traded services with printers and copiers in exchange for cash and other resources that I then used to obtain production gear and equipment. Whatever skills that you have, understand, there is a need somewhere for them. I've seen cats hand out promotional flyers for used gear shops, in exchange for discounts on gear and musical equipment.

Getting Your Gear Summary

Looking back on my first recording session, that engineer really didn't know much about sampling. But he knew more than I did. He also knew **Gear-Capability™**. He shot off a list of different pieces of gear and equipment, along with its capabilities, it's prices, who used it, and where I could get it. So, what was the result of that $700.00 session? *The result was that I got a number of tips about different gear and equipment.* But more importantly, I gained a better idea of which gear was right for me. The other positive effect from that session was that I created a powerful contact.

Notes

BeatTip™

"Listen, if at all possible, I recommend recording some sessions at a professional (commercial) recording studio where your favorite producer or producers have been known to record. I've created a lot of contacts from the studios that I've recorded in. I've also acquired a lot of tips... In some cases I got the tips, while these producers were actually there!"

Finally, realize one thing. The gear and equipment that you first choose to use, MAY NOT be your final production setup. Your development as a producer will dictate what you continue to use and what you decide not to use. I produced on an E-Mu SP 1200/Akai S950 setup for three years, before I finally realized and admitted to myself that it would never compliment the sound that I was trying to achieve. It took me another year before I actually made that change! For real, do not hesitate to change your production setup if you feel that it isn't working for you...

You have to decide if you feel more comfortable working with a classic setup, like an Akai S950/Akai MPC 60II; or a contemporary setup, like a Korg Triton Keyboard/Akai MPC 2000XL. Whatever decision you make, consider the fact that an overwhelming majority of current and new producers typically use contemporary setups. (see MusicStudy™: Music Theory section for more on classic and contemporary production setups).

Notes

SAMPLING

O.K., LET THIS BE KNOWN: most producers, particularly, the die-hard "non-sampling" producers, fail to realize that **Sampling**[1] has been a part of the music recording process for over 25 years! It became the basis for the production of Hip Hop-Rap Beats and Music in the mid-1980s, and in my opinion, it received it's biggest creative boom during the early to mid-1990s. Now, due to a number of factors, such as the widespread "biting" and lazy "copying" of production styles, the emergence of "do-it-all" electronic instruments—full of a large number of already-edited instrumentals and sounds, and the commercial onslaught of keyboard-based beats[2], the art of sampling has been reduced from its once mighty role. However, there is still a number of well-known, and crititcally proven producers who still use, and in fact feature, record samples as the basis for their beat and music production.

Sampling on the Akai S950

Every digital sampler has a sampling section; however, the mode in which you actually sample may vary in name. Generally, on the older hardware samplers, the names will have something to do with the word Recording. On the Akai S950, you do your sampling in the REC mode.

BeatTip™

Naming Your Sample

Before you sample *anything*, especially drum sounds, I recommend giving your samples simple, short names that you can easily identify with. For example, if you already have 20 snare samples, you might simply name the next one: Snare 21. Don't get into elaborate names for your sounds because you will be using them often and rapidly, in the development of new beats. Nearly every producer that I know, (that is not getting paid for their production services), have very long, elaborate names for their sampled drum sounds. For instance, names like: Crazy Snare and Hardcore Kick, are too descriptive. Plus you'll come

---

[1] **Sampling** — The digital recording of a musical or sound phrase, that can then be edited and reproduced. For example, a musical or sound phrase that is originally recorded by a device such as a CD recorder, is only a recorded reproduction. However, a musical or sound phrase that is "sampled" can be changed from its original recording. For instance, the phrase can be extended or shortened. A sample can be anything from a broken bottle to a bass guitar.

[2] Keyboard-Based Beats — Beats that are made using keyboards, rather than dedicated samplers. Typically, they feature simple keyboard patterns and no record samples.

Notes

to view these sounds only for how they're described; and thus you'll overlook each sound's full potential. On the other hand, most well-known producers have a simple system for naming their sampled drum sounds. And keep in mind, when you eventually go to track your sounds at either your home pre-production studio or at a larger, commercial recording studio, the engineer will simply name a kick a kick, a snare a snare, a hat a hat, etc. Get the point!

BeatTip™

Two overlooked, but very important pages in the REC mode are: the **Audio Source** page and the **Audio Bandwidth** page. The Audio Source page is where you select the source from which you will be sampling from. You can choose from: Analog Input (1), Digital Fibre Optic (2), or Phono (3). (On many different samplers, these are the exact three choices).

Typically, many producers select Phono (3). ***NEVER DO THIS!*** Always select Analog Input (1) and leave it as your default for everything that you intend to sample.[3] Samplers are ALL digital, despite any myth to the contrary… Some samplers are "warmer" sounding than others, but they all process sounds "warm" when the settings are set to analog. Also, you should run your turntable, CD player and cassette deck through a DJ mixer. From there, it's up to you how you want to route it to the S950. (I RUN EVERYTHING THROUGH THE S950). If you have a Mixing Board, you can send a direct out to the S950s Line input. You can also simply send a cable from your DJ mixer's SEND output into the S950's LINE input. This really depends on how much you want to E.Q. the sounds before you sample them. In other words, this a personal sound quality issue. Every producer has a different opinion about E.Q.ing the intended sample.

The **Audio Bandwidth** page is where you select the bandwidth or **frequency response level**[4]. On the S950, the selectable bandwidth range is 3000Hz to 19200Hz. The higher the bandwidth setting, the brighter the sample will sound and vice-versa. Keep in mind though, the higher you set the bandwidth, the more sample memory you will use up. Even still, I suggest finding a comfortable

---

[3]Point is, most typical setups, producers RARELY sample "directly" from the turntable (phono) out directly into a sampler. Instead, the turntable runs through a DJ/Stereo Mixer, EQ, or some other processing and/or effects device. In turn, the DJ/Stereo Mixer's (or whatever device's) SEND output would be connected to your sampler's Line Input.

[4] A higher Audio Bandwidth setting, or rather higher frequency response level, will make the sample sound brighter. But remember, this takes up more memory than lower Audio Bandwidth settings. The frequency response level is one of the things that separate the Akai S950 from the E-Mu SP 1200. Although both units are 12-bit, the Akai S950 has a higher (range) frequency response level. And thus, sounds have a bigger, warmer over all sound.

Notes

high-level setting, somewhere between 15000Hz and 16000Hz[5], and leave it as your default setting for **everything** that you sample, especially drum sounds. Sometimes it's also a good idea to take the settings up higher for some drum or percussion sounds, i.e., hi-hats and closed snares. Higher settings will give sounds compression-like effects! But remember to return the setting back to your default.

"The reason that you should have a default bandwidth setting is because it allows you to customize and uniform all of your sounds. This is absolutely key in creating, customizing and developing your own overall unique production sound and style."

    I DO NOT RECOMMEND having different bandwidth settings for everything that you sample. Don't get me wrong, you won't disrupt anything if you do use different settings. It's just more time consuming, and it doesn't help you to unify your sound. However, if you do ultimately decide to use different audio bandwidth settings, at least make those the default settings for the sounds that you sample. For example, *always* use the same bandwidth setting for deep, hard kicks, or thick bass lines, etc. Another plus to having a default setting for the bandwidth is that it saves you a lot of production time. It allows you to sample sounds more quickly and efficiently. It also familiarizes you with what works, like how certain sounds should be sampled, and then edited.

Sampling Vinyl Records, Cassettes, and CDs

    The biggest, most overwhelmingly popular form of Sampling in Hip Hop-Rap still involves sampling vinyl records!
    There are two ways you can approach sampling records (as well as cassettes and CDs): **SpotSampling™** and **Full-Listen™ Sampling**. SpotSampling™ is the process of randomly checking over a record for certain breaks, parts or grooves. When I first started producing, that's all I did. I think I spent three years like this, word up. I would buy new records and just skim over them until somethin' "popped out". I learned a lot about intros and outros, but that's about it. I assumed that this was how most producers did it. I thought, "Who had time to actually listen to entire albums?". Then I learned... SpotSampling™ is helpful if you're already familiar with the record that you're intending to sample from. Like if you're looking for keys or strings, or even a

---

[5] 15000Hz and 16000Hz will produce a fuller, more out front sound. 9000Hz-13000Hz will produce a dominant, warm sound.

Notes

drum sound. However, **DO NOT SpotSample™ a record, cassette, or CD that you've never heard before.** *There's way too much that you will definitely miss!*

**"Whenever you get new records, etc. give it a Full-Listen.
Listen to everything. Do not skim or skip ahead!"**

BeatTip™

To really understand Sampling, you have to gain a "feel" for what you should listen and look for. You can sample pieces and phrases as you listen, but don't skip ahead. You really can't gain a feel for a record's mood in that manner. I've known a lot of producers who simply try to listen to the intro and outros of songs, just as I did when I started producing. In fact, a lot of producers still shop and "dig" for records in this fashion. They go to used record stores, select a few records, then check them out on the store's turntable. **DO NOT EVER DO THIS**.

Listen, whenever you're in a record store, digging for vinyl, be quick with your decisions. When you pick out an album, if the name of the artist or the album cover catches your interest, just get the album (provided you can *pay* for it). Thoroughly check it out when you get it back home. The idea is, *when you go to a used record store, just dig and leave!* Surprises, or better yet, good musical "accidents" are only found in the process of your personal production practice, word up. In my opinion, testing records, while in the record store, offers too many other people the chance to hear what you're considering. Some other producers (in the store at that time) may try and convince you that the record you are considering has been "used" already by other established producers, just to stop you from buying it. As soon as you put that record down, they pick it up *and Buy it*.

One more thing about diggin' for records. You should always go for albums first, over 45s. Albums are a much better value and investment. They contain a consistent "feel and mood" that you can't really pick up with just an A & B side 45. Also, you can return to an album much more than you can a single.

Check This Out:

When you really dig into a song on a record, by giving it that full-listen, you catch all sorts of interesting things. I remember listening to this one song by **The Intruders,** that I actually probably listened to well over 50 times

Notes

before…Anyway, during this one practice session, I heard a mistake. It was a minor, however, noticeable, vocal mistake…But the point is, *they kept the take!* Why didn't they (**Gamble and Huff**, the producers of the song; **the engineer**, and **The Intruders**, themselves) simply re-track the vocals? Because they understood that they couldn't "re-track" *the mood!* Well, that's like sampling. The idea is to sample the "feel and mood" of a song. Also, when you really listen to a song, you learn how it was arranged. By getting a feeling for the song and understanding its arrangement, you'll know how to sample, "chop" and loop it. I once studied, for 3 months, the tendencies of James Brown's standard intro, verse, and bridge patterns. By getting a feel for how James Brown arranged his compositions, I gained an excellent understanding of Sampling and Sample Editing!

A Full-Listen™ is also better because it helps you to catalogue usable sounds in your head. For instance, what happens when you have "that sound" in your head but you can't quite call it. Your catalogue memory of records will help you get it out. Or if you need some keys, horns, violins, strings, etc., you'll know which records to go to.

Complete Phrase™ and SparePart Phrase™

I break everything down into phrases. When you listen to a record, cassette or CD, the songs are made up from a combination of a number of varying musical phrases.[6] I divide these phrases into two categories: **Complete Phrases**™ and **SparePart Phrases**™.

A Complete Phrase (or full musical pattern) is like a short story. It has a beginning, a middle and an end. Usually, they're made up of two or more bars, but there are also some that come in the one bar variety. Think of Complete Phrases like ready-made loops. They are usually very easy to identify. And thus, they are easier to sample and loop. This is why the overwhelming majority of producers dig for Complete Phrases. But always remember this, If you're gonna' sample a Complete Phrase, the more rare the record that you're sampling from, the better! Sample clearance is now a major area in the Music Recording Business. So, realize that, if you sample a very identifiable or well-known Complete Phrase, expect to pay to get that sample cleared. (Unless you're fortunate enough to sell the beat to an established recording artist. In that case, let the artist's label handle the sample clearing headache).

---

[6] A Musical Phrase is simply any musical pattern, like: Kick – Kick – Snare – Kick – Kick – Snare… and so on.

Notes

_____

_____

_____

_____

_____

_____

_____

_____

_____

_____

_____

_____

_____

_____

BeatTip™

Sampling SparePart Phrases™ is a little more difficult, a LOT more involved, but much more rewarding, word up. SparePart Phrases™ are simply pieces of the larger Complete Phrase. (Now you see why giving each song a Full Listen is important.) See, once you get a feel for a song, you can begin to catch the SpareParts or pieces of the *whole story*. The pieces often stand alone like great dialogue. In fact, the pieces will often signal where you can and should take the direction of the new beat itself! Indeed, you can then take those phrases or pieces and turn them into your own new Complete Phrase(s). Sampling SparePart Phrases™ is usually more rewarding. For one thing, the phrases or pieces that you sample won't be nearly as easy to identify as the original Complete Phrase, and thus you will avoid having to pay to clear the samples. Another benefit of SpartePart Phrase™ sampling is that it will train and develop your musical ear and overall understanding of rhythm arrangements and drum & loop programming.

"Consider this: a number of classic beats, produced by many of the production pioneers, were actually created from *one sample*! The more experienced Hip Hop-Rap producers are skilled at one-sample beats. They know how to copy and manipulate one sample to the point where the original sample is unrecognizable, even though the original "mood" and integrity is still left in tact…

SparePart Phrase™ sampling will always allow you to create challenging, riveting beats; even from the shortest and simplest of samples."

BeatTip™

Sample *EVERYTHING*, especially your drums, through the Akai S950. (Or whatever stand alone sampler that you have). *ONLY USE THE AKAI MPC 60II AS A SEQUENCER!* (Or whatever stand alone sequencer that you have).

As crazy as this may sound, in my opinion, this is the absolute best way to use the Akai MPC 60II. There is one well-known, very respected producer

Notes

_____

_____

_____

_____

_____

_____

_____

_____

_____

_____

_____

_____

_____

_____

who also uses the MPC60II/S950 in this manner. (I'm not blowing up any names, but you definitely know this DJ). You see, most producers who have the MPC 60II use it to sample drums. There's nothing wrong with that, you'll still get a good sound. But this takes up more of your time programming and reassigning drum pads. By sampling everything through the S950, then sequencing it all on the MPC 60II, you have a superior control over the programming of the complete beat. Everything is simple and easy, and unified: **One unit to sample, chop, and edit. Another unit to shape, loop, and pitch.** I do not recommend sampling anything with the MPC 60II. The sound combination of the Akai S950/MPC 60II works better when you use the S950 as your dedicated sampler and the MPC 60II as your dedicated sequencer. Technically, I don't know why, I think it has to do with the sound exciter of the MPC 60II...but I really don't care! The point is, I do know that the overall sound is warmer, biggerand more dominant, when you use the MPC 60II/S950 setup in this manner.

Note.

If you do not have an Akai S950, that's O.K., just make sure that whatever sampler that you use is your dedicated sampler for EVERYTHING THAT YOU SAMPLE. Do not get caught up in sampling drums and bass on one unit, then keys and horns on another unit! Sample ALL sounds through the same unit. This will not only organize and unify your own unique sound, it will also train your ear for mixing.

Notes

SAMPLE EDITING

FIRST LET ME SAY THIS. **When you buy some new gear, the instructional manual that is included mentions Sample Editing, but it doesn't say *anything* substantial about making Hip Hop-Rap Beats and Music! Equipment manuals are written in a technical language, for a primarily technical consumer. When I first started buying and using gear, no one told me how technically profound I would need to become. For example, I didn't know that "chopping" actually meant editing and truncating, and so forth. Either way, I finally realized that one of my biggest problems was the fact that I didn't really seek out production help. I thought that a "real" producer discovered everything on his own. The reality is, "real" producers get tips... I was surprised when I learned how two of the main Hip Hop-Rap pioneers actually taught each other their techniques.**

Now, let's get into Sample Editing...

Once you're satisfied with what you've sampled, you have to edit it. On the Akai S950 you edit your samples in the EDIT SAMPLE mode. In this mode, there are a number of ways that you can edit your samples. You can copy your samples; you can stretch the time length of your samples; you can reverse the playback of your samples; you can even re-sample your samples at lower bandwidths[1]. Among the many pages in the EDIT SAMPLE mode, the two most critical pages are: the Start Point and End Point pages. It is in the Start and End Point pages where you will actually do the most "chopping" of your samples.

Simply put, **Chopping** is the process of removing or trimming unwanted sections from a sample. Usually, it involves trimming sections from the start and end of a sample. But as your skills develop, you will definitely chop and manipulate various sections of a sample. Also remember that: when you playback your samples on a MIDI Sequencer or Keyboard, you want that exact-touch crispness. To achieve this, you have to chop your samples down to pinpoint precision.

BeatTip™

Here's the best rule for precision chopping on the Akai S950: tap the P.B (Play Back) button, repeatedly until the sound plays on the hit of your fingertip.

---

[1] Although lowering the bandwidth setting conserves memory, it also decreases the brightness of the sound being sampled.

Notes

If the sound is not falling on the hit of your fingertip, then you need to chop (cut) the **Start Point** of the sample some more, until it does! If the **End Point** carries over longer than you want it to, then you need to chop the End Point of the sample, until it stops where you want it to. The idea is to tap, not to hold the P.B button when you're first chopping the sample. By holding the P.B too long, you will get an inaccurate starting point. After you establish the right starting point, then you can hold the P.B down. This allows you to play back the sample, so that you can capture the right End Point.

Keep in mind, chopping drum sounds is more straight forward than any other sounds. However, when you chop phrases you have to be more careful. Reason, being, the Start and End points of a phrase have the power to off-set any drum timing. That is, the precision chopping of a phrase is critical for different reasons. The phrase will actually play "over" the drums. So, if the hit of the phrase is off a little, not hitting on that pinpoint accuracy, it will make the entire drum program and/or loop sequence sound off. (see more on looping in the Sequencing: Looping section).

Note.

If you use another sampler other than the Akai S950, simply apply the above techniques to your unit. The mode or name where you manipulate sample length may vary in your unit's menu heading, but the aforementioned techniques should be applied universally, whenever you are sample editing.

FILTERING

After you've chopped your sample down to the desired length, you have to filter it. Filtering your samples is just as critical as chopping them. On the Akai S950, filtering takes place in the **EDIT PROGRAM** mode. I find that filtering is often overlooked. A lot of producers choose not to filter their drum sounds as much as they do their other sounds. This neglect, in filtering drum sounds, usually results in flat sounding drums. For this reason and more, I not only recommend that you filter your drum sounds, I suggest that you start there first!

Notes

BeatTip™

DRUMS pt. 1

The three main drum sounds are: **Kick**, **Snare** and **Hat**. *You should filter each one of these very distinct drum sounds in a separate fashion.* Kicks should be filtered with a lot of low to mid frequency. That is, you start from the low, (on the Akai S950, 0 being the lowest, 99 being the highest) and work up to the mid frequencies, being careful not to go into the highs (80+)! You **rarely** want your kicks to have high frequency. Too much high frequency will make your kicks sound soft and/or distorted. On the other hand, a good low on your kicks will give 'em that commanding, driving sound. If you want your kicks to really bang (not punch), you have to practice "manipulating the lows". (for more on filtering drums, see the Sequencing and Mixing sections).

Snares should be filtered with a lot of mid to high frequency. However, be careful not to "max-out the highs" on your snares. That is, be very careful not to add too much high frequency. Even though it's sometimes cool to have your snares tear through, you do not ever want them to dominate the entire beat. In my opinion, snares get far too much attention in today's Hip Hop-Rap production. In most cases, really like 9 out of 10 times, they are *over processed*; in particular, over compressed! Unneeded compression can be avoided by proper and efficient filtering and a little reverb, or maybe some delay effects.

You should filter your hats and cymbals similar to how you filter your snares. However, with hats and shakers, sometimes it's all right to add more high frequency. The added high brightens up the overall sound and it let's the hat "steady" the pace of the beat. It smoothes out the beat's entire high-end.

Notes

BeatTip™

"It is absolutely critical to leave all of your drum sound settings as default settings. These settings, taken together, will be your most important Default Set Combination.[2]"

At this time I think it's important to mention that too many drums is never a good thing. I know producers who brag about having hundreds of snares, and in fact, hundreds of other drum sounds, as well. This is too much! With so many different drum sounds you can't really unify or develop your own production sound. The development of a unique production sound is based on familiarity. A producer's sound should be a familiar signature. From Rap to Rock, producers and engineers ALWAYS work from preset mixing boards[3], especially for the recording of drums. Too many drums sounds will most likely hamper your development and maintenance of a consistent sound. The idea is to have a reasonable, manageable number of drums. If there's a need for an adjustment, you can manipulate your sounds in the chopping and filtering phases or the mixing phase. Creative mixing can make 1 drum kick sound like 10 different ones.

Also, it's not practical to have too many drum sounds. **"Quality production is efficient production."**™ A large part of efficiency deals with the rate at which you can produce new beats. I'm not saying that the best beats are made in 10 minutes or an hour, or a day. Every producer has their own "perfection level". What I am saying is that, in order for you to produce at a reasonably quick turnover rate, you absolutely have to have *manageable* drum sounds. Pre-set drum sequences (see Sequencing section) are one of the most important keys to an efficient production turnover rate. And these sequences are interdependent upon having a solid core of drum sounds. The core number of drums that you keep is entirely up to you. I recommend carrying no more than 5 kicks, 10 snares, and 15 hats. The less drum sounds you keep, the better. This

---

[2] **A Default Set Combination is a group of default settings that combine to work together. For instance, when you edit each sample, patterns will emerge as to how you want particular samples to sound. Your preferences for how you like your kicks, snares, hats, and other samples to sound will dictate how you edit them. After you establish default settings, that is, the editing parameters from which you always begin for each kind of sample, you actually create Default Set Combinations. Keeping the same settings**
for the same kinds of samples, particularly drum samples, allows you to easily track which combinations work best.

[3] **ALL established producers track and mix on preset boards. What this means is, that they have default settings for the faders and EQs on every channel that they use. In other words, they have preset EQs for all of their drum sounds. Any and all adjustments are made from these presets.**

Notes

_____

_____

_____

_____

_____

_____

_____

_____

_____

_____

_____

_____

_____

_____

increases your chances of storing them as default sounds in your Akai S950 (or other sampler), as opposed to having too many unused, and unnecessary drum sample disks. But 1 or 2 drum sample disks (full of assorted kicks, snares, hats, and other sounds) on standby is cool…100 is ridiculous.

BeatTip™

One way to narrow down your drums is to chart them. At one time I actually had over 300 separate drum sounds, then I narrowed it down to about 30. What I did was practice making beats with various drum patterns and drum sound combinations, like snare 12, kick 8, hat 2. Then I charted the tempos that I used these combinations in. I taped these charts on the wall, directly behind where I sat in my production area. This way, all I needed to do was turn around and locate a combination. After some time, I was able to determine which combinations blended best. And many practice sessions later, I was able to memorize every combination that I liked. These blends and combinations became the default rhythm sections for my production. So, whenever a drum sound didn't fit my range of tempos, or the way in which I liked my rhythm sections to swing, I simply deleted it and removed it from the chart. This is how I got rid of a lot of unnecessary drum sounds. What I gained was my own, consistent (very manageable) sound.

FILTERING OUT BASS

Ever wonder how some producers' beats have that thick, driving bass line? A lot of producers wrongly believe that this can only be achieved by using a Bass Novation or various sound modules. Fact is, there's really only three ways to get those powerful, warm bass parts.

1.) You can hire a session bass player and have 'em play the bass part of a particular sample, then compress and boost the low up in the mix.

2.) You can sample the bass directly (played live or recorded), then again, compress and boost the low up in the mix.

3.) You can sample the bass from a Keyboard and/or Sound Module, then filter, compress and/or add other effects.

Notes

4.)   You can sample from off a record, then filter out the bass. And then again, compress and boost the low up in the mix. (Keep in mind, your skills at sample filtering will determine how much processing you will need to apply in the mix).

BeatTip™

The simplest way to filter out a bass line and/or part from a sample is to turn the filtering down to 0 and work upwards until the bass sound is "out" in front and driving. But be careful! If you filter too low, you can muffle and distort the bass.

Here is the detailed explanation for the best way to filter out the bass on an Akai S950.[4]

- In the EDIT PROGRAM mode, locate the sample that you want the bass filtered out on.
- Go to the Keygroup page (page 03).
- Where it says Copy (+), enter the (+) sign.
  This will copy the entire Keygroup, sample, filtering parameters, assigned output channel and all.
- Locate the new Keygroup and assign it to a different channel, preferably the channel/output on the mixing board that is next to the channel/output of the high part of the sample. Then set the filter on the new Keygroup to 0.
- Now, when you strike the assigned pad on your MPC 60II (or other MIDI Sequencing Device), you will actually trigger two sounds simultaneously. You'll have both a mid to high sound and a low sound of the exact same sample.
- On your mixing board, you simply mix the low part with a little more bottom, being careful to keep it warm. On the other hand, you mix the mid to high part with some high, a little more mid and nearly no low at all.
  The proper blend will effectively filter out the Bass. (Of course, sound taste will vary with each producer).

---

[4] If you do not have an Akai S950, simply apply the "copying and filtering" techniques, hereby explained.

Notes

_____

_____

_____

_____

_____

_____

_____

_____

_____

_____

_____

_____

_____

Keys, Strings and Other Highs

Generally, the best way to filter out strings and keyboard parts and other sounds that naturally carry high frequency is to work from high-mid to high. That is, start at about 70 and work up to 99.

NOTE. If you're using a unit other than an Akai S950, just work between the top third of your unit's allowable values (levels), and work your way up.

Notes

SEQUENCING & PROGRAMMING: The Mid-Game of Making a Beat

**You've sampled your sounds. You've chopped and filtered them...
Now it's time to "complete the beat".™**

All Digital MIDI Samplers have functions specifically for sample placement. Sample Placement is simply the process of mapping samples out across the pads of a MIDI Sequencer/Drum Machine; or across keys, in the case of a keyboard or MIDI keyboard controller. Each MIDI device may have a different name for this function in the menu heading. For instance, the Akai S950 uses KEYGROUPS.

In order for you to playback a sample or a sound on your MIDI Sequencer's pads or keys, samples must be mapped out. To do this in the Akai S950, you must first assign each one of your samples to a KEYGROUP. In the EDIT PROGRAM mode, the KEYGROUP range on the S950 is from c0 to G8. Each KEYGROUP denotes the pitch at which each sample will be played back.

BeatTip™

Set the pitch for KEYGROUP 1 as the same as the default pitch that you sample all of your sounds.

That is, in REC mode, on the page: **Pitch of sound being recorded.** Whatever you choose as your default setting, also choose as your default setting for KEYGROUP 1. This way, all you need to do is move chronologically as you assign new samples to new KEYGROUPS. What I mean is this. If KEYGROUP 1 reads: C3 60, (the 60 representing notes up to 127), then KEYGROUP 3 should read like this: d3 62. You can now assign these KEYGROUPS to the drum pads of the Akai MPC 60II (or whatever Sequencer/Drum Machine that you are using),

Notes

following an easy chronological order. For instance, the Perc 1 pad on the MPC 60 II can be C3 60, and the Perc 3 pad can be d3 62.

It's not as complex as it might first seem, but it gets real crazy and very time consuming, if you try to operate without default KEYGROUP settings. This is why I advise mapping out[1] the simplest KEYGROUP setting that you possibly can.

BeatTip™

Group Map Assignments™ (GMA)

Depending on what Sequencer/Drum Machine that you're using, the names of the pads may be different. So you should develop your own preference for which pads you want to use to trigger sounds. See, on the entire MPC Series (MPC 60, 60 II, 3000, 2000, 2000XL, and so forth), there are 16 total pads, laid out as 4 rows of 4 individual drum pads. This is actually the standard number of pads and layout for most top rate Drum Machine/Sequencers. So, the names (or numbers) of the individual pads, like Perc 3, are not important when you're mapping out samples from other samplers, sound modules and/or keyboards. You do not have to assign a percussion sound to a pad named Perc. You can assign ANY sound to ANY pad. It's your preference: top row, middle rows, bottom row, it's up to you. However, whatever you decide to do, I strongly recommend that you assign your sounds into *Group Map Assignments*.

For example, your base drum sounds: kicks, snares, and hats, should be assigned to neighboring pads. Having your main kick sound on the 3rd pad top row, your main snare on the 4th pad of a middle row; and your main hat on the 1st pad, bottom row isn't very practical for programming your base drum sequences. When you're programming the core structure of the drum sequence, an assignment like this would require your fingers to travel too far, too quickly. This increases the probability that you're timing will be off, or at the least, it will make it difficult for you to get the timing down that you *really* want. On the other hand, if you assign your pads in groups, especially your main drum sounds, you gain a number of advantages.

The most obvious advantage of Group Map Assignments is the proximity of the pads and the sounds that they are triggering. That is, the closer the pads

---

[1] Mapping Out. The process of assigning sounds to the pads of your drum machine. For keyboards, the process of assigning sounds to the keys.

Notes

(sounds) that you wanna' use (in conjunction) are to one another, the easier it will be for you to go from one pad to another. Instead of making pad-strikes that force you to go from like row 4 back to row 1, you can simply assign the sounds of that *group* to either row 1 or row 4. The idea is to narrow down your Group Map Assignments to 3 or 4 pads in a group. For drums, this is easy. Kick, snare, hat are a natural group, so keep them that way. You can add any other drum-related sound to this group to make it a 4-pad group, taking up one entire row of pads… simple, plain, easy and organized!

The biggest advantage of Group Map Assignments is rhythm organization. That is, by mapping your sounds out into groups, you are in essence, turning your Sequencer/Drum Machine into a rhythm section: the drummer (or drum GMA) is on one row; the bassist (or bass GMA) is on another row; the guitarist (or guitar GMA) is on another row; and the pianist (or piano/strings GMA) is on another row. Here, it's important to point out that, the kind of production we're talking about is fundamentally electronic and/or digital, understand, there's no getting around that! However, my perspective is that, as the producer/ programmer, YOU are the rhythm section. I believe that a Hip Hop-Rap producer's musical understanding is just as relevant as a traditional musician's understanding. The ONLY difference is that most Hip Hop-Rap producers do not play "traditional" musical instruments, (though this trend is changing, as more and more producers are becoming trained with traditional instruments, like piano and bass). Whatever you sample and chop is up to you; likewise how you choose to program and sequence these samples (put it all together) is also up to you. In this light, the Sequencers/Drum Machines and/or Samplers that you use are indeed musical instruments!

BeatTip™

TIMING CORRECT

Once your KEYGROUPS are set, and you have the sounds triggering from their assigned drum pads, you're ready to continue. First, go to the TIMING CORRECT button, and set the proper value…

Have you ever tapped in a drum pattern on your drum machine and/or sequencer and it didn't play back *exactly* how you programmed it? Well, that's because the Timing Correct value "corrected" your timing. That is, it placed the

Notes

sound or sounds that you tapped in to the nearest corrected note. The overwhelming majority of producers set the note value at 1/16 Note or 1/16 TRPLT. I warn you, if you are not particularly skilled at note correction and the like, DO NOT SET THE TIMING CORRECT at 1/16 Note or 1/16 TRPLT. Your drum programs will result in a "stuck" or slow sound, with an off-swing.

In Timing Correct mode, on the MPC 60II, (or E-Mu SP1200, or any other Sequencer) *set your note value at 1/32 TRPLT, and leave it as your default.* All other note values will "correct" your timing. You shouldn't use corrected timing *or* the metronome, for that matter. It's better to be able to program your drum sequences exactly how and when your fingers hit the pads, mistakes and all… And you should develop the ability to record your programs by ear. That is, you should get accustomed to programming sequences WITHOUT using the metronome for timing. Too much reliability on the metronome will hamper your programming development. Also, set the Shuffle % to: 50, and set the Shift timing to: LATER.

After you've set the most effective Timing Correct value (that works best for you), you're ready to create a sequence. The default setting for an open or empty sequence on an Akai MPC 60II is: one bar, set at a tempo of 30bpm. When you start a brand new sequence, the easiest thing to do is to record the main sample into an empty or default sequence. Press **STEP EDIT** and simply tap the main sample (drum sound, bass part, loop, etc.) into an open sequence. Next, go to tempo, and adjust it (increase/decrease it) until the sequence loops itself where you want it to. If you tap in a loop, it's good to tempo the sequence until the sample loops exactly where you want it to. This way, you put the drums in over the top. Or you can tap in the drums sounds, tempo the sequence, and then put the main sample over the top of the drums. This is key because it keeps you aware of how rhythm sections actually work. (*Note. The majority of producers loop their samples **before** they record or program them into a sequence. This is O.K., but I recommend looping the sample live, in real time*).

To increase the length of any sequence, simply copy the entire sequence to itself. Check it out, if the main sample is two bars in length, you can simply double the sequence up! In other words, you simply duplicate (copy) the sequence so that it's a two bar *sequence*. This is very important because most main samples (the primary grooves and/or loops) are either 2 or 4 bars. What I mean is, when you sample something from a record, let's say an intro, that intro is usually 4 to 8 bars. Chopped in half, that same sample takes up 2 to 4 bars of sequencing length! So, with this understanding, you know that most Hip Hop-

Notes

_____

_____

_____

_____

_____

_____

_____

_____

_____

_____

_____

_____

_____

_____

Rap beats are built upon a basic 2-bar or 4-bar platform. (See the Beat Structure: Basics and Manipulation section for an in-depth explanation of this).

You can also adjust the tempo on an empty sequence to the desired **BPM**[2], then copy the sequence *before* you record in (tap in) a sound. Although there are MANY quality hardware sequencers and software sequencing options, I find that the MPC 60II's sequencer **is the best and easiest that I have ever used**. When a sequence is playing, you can record in real-time, right over the top. All you have to do is press and hold down the OVER DUB button, then press and hold down the PLAY button. When the red lights above each of these buttons appear, you are in record mode, even though the sequence is actually playing. This is real-time recording.[3]

BeatTip™

Whether you use an Akai MPC 60II as your sequencer or not, in my opinion, it is not only easier to loop your sounds through the sequencer, it's more effective. By looping your samples using the sequencer, in real-time, I feel that you gain more control over the structure of the beat. I know a number of quality producers who loop their samples before they sequence them. That's o.k., but the samples' potential isn't totally achieved in this manner. What I mean is, when you begin to try things out, by having the sample looped already, you can't really hear what it sounds like looped from different end points. However, by sequencing or what I call "tempo-ing your loop"™, you can hear how the sample sounds—with *unintended end points*—as you manipulate the tempo of the loop. A lot of good beats and music will come from how well you capture and redirect your "unintended" accidents.

After you've programmed your main sample into a sequence and you got it looping at that right tempo, play the sequence and program your drum sounds in, right over the top of the sample, in real time. The result of everything together, moving right and at the desired tempo, is the *primary theme loop* or simply, *primary loop*. This is extremely important because the primary theme loop will be the basis from which you build ALL of your beats into actual songs! *A note about sequencers.*

---

[2] **BPM** stands for Beats Per Minute.
[3] Real-time recording can be performed on nearly ALL hardware and/or software sequencers. This type of programming is standard, but how well you understand this will determine the development of your real-time recording skill.

Notes

Now, the Akai MPC 60II has 99 individual tracks. Some sequencers have more, some have less. I've heard all sorts of reasons as to why you should give each one of your sounds it's own track; most notably, because it makes it easier to correct your mistakes. Producer/Engineer conventional wisdom says: Kick on track 1, Snare on track 2, Hat on track 3, Bass part on track 4, etc. To me, if you already have a mixing console or access to one, programming sounds on different tracks in the MPC is not necessary or *practical*. For example, Let's say that you program a Hi-Hat wrong on the first quarter note of the 2nd bar. Just to remove that one incorrectly programmed hi-hat, you have to go to track 4. But if everything is on the same track, you simply take out the unwanted hi-hat when it comes up in the sequence (around in the loop)! My point is, when you make mistakes, you're gonna' have to remove the sound from its incorrect place, *anyway*. So, the only thing I've ever noticed about placing all of your sounds on individual tracks, within a sequence, is that it takes up more programming time. If you wanna' hear your sounds soloed as they play, solo them on your mixing board. The best thing to do is to program all of your samples and sounds on the same track. Keep it simple, keep it easy. The *only* time that you should put your sounds on separate individual tracks is when you are tracking them for recording and mixing. (Remember, here I'm only talking about **tracks on the Akai MPC 60II**, not channels. When recording and mixing, you want your sounds to be separated by different channels on the Akai S950—or whatever sampler that you have—especially if your sampler has multiple direct outputs. You would send the signals from these multiple outputs to the separate channels on the mixing console. In turn, the channels from the mixing console would be sent to separate individual tracks for recording. Thereby making the whole mixing and recording process much more fluid and efficient).

BeatTip™

I should point out however, that if you are using a Sampler or Sequencer that does NOT have multiple individual outs, then it may be to your advantage to program your sounds on multiple tracks. For synths and workstations, this is usually the way to do it. The only problem here though is that it takes more time to track (record) the instrumental this way, than if you were able to assign sounds to multiple individual outs.

If you are using multiple tracks, the best way to track your instrumentals is to pan (hard-turn the audio signal from stereo to mono) each track to the left

Notes

or the right. This way, instead of tracking one sound at a time, you are able to track two sounds at a time, using the Left/Right outputs of whatever unit you are using!

Beat Structure: The Basic Components

The basic structure of ANY contemporary song with vocals, whether it be the Blues, Jazz, Soul, Rock, Hip Hop-Rap, etc. contains any number or combination of the following components:

Intro; Verse; Chorus (Hook); Bridge; Outro. These components are often then arranged in the following chronological structure:

1. Intro; 2. Verse 1; 3. Chorus (Hook); 4. Verse 2; 5. Bridge; 6. Verse 3; 7. Outro.

Each of these components are made by instituting a *"change"* in the **primary loop**. (A change can be anything from a kick-snare pattern, alternating on the first and second bars). The theme loop is what I call the most-used part of the beat; the part of the beat that the verse vocals ride over! In other words, the theme loop is actually the **Verse** component of a Hip Hop-Rap beat. The purpose of the Verse component is to serve as the driving platform for the verse vocals.

The **Intro** component of a beat is where any of the initial adlib vocals go. The Intro component consists of the verse component minus or plus "something". This "something" can be a whole variety of things, word up—anything from extra sounds floating over the top of the theme loop, to sounds actually muted or taken out of the theme loop! When intros are used in Hip Hop-Rap, more than often they are made up of the theme loop, minus some sounds; maybe a kick, or hat, sometimes even the main bass part. The purpose of the Intro is to pull the listener in, by giving them a hint of the composition that is about to proceed.

The **Chorus** component of a beat is where the chorus vocals (or rather hook vocals) ride! Like the Intro, the chorus component consists of the verse component, minus or plus "something". Again, this "something" can be an assortment of features: from extra sounds floating over the top, to sounds actually muted or taken out! The chorus part in most Hip Hop-Rap beats almost always keeps the verse part in tact; with additional sounds, like strings, keys, or horns, complimenting it. Sometimes there are more involved changes, but for the most

Notes

part, the drum program stays pretty much the same. The Chorus (Hook) component is the *secondary theme loop* because it is the second most used part of the entire beat, after the Verse part! The purpose of the Chorus (Hook) component is to serve as the driving platform for the chorus (commonly referred to as The Hook) vocals.

The new trend in Hip Hop-Rap over the past several years is the non-use of the **Bridge** component. Even still, I believe that producers should be aware of what it is and how effectively it can be used. Just as with the Intro and Outro components, the Bridge is based on the primary theme loop. However, the purpose of the Bridge is not always as straight forward. What I mean is, the Bridge has the special power to do two things to a beat: it can serve as an interesting intermission, but more importantly, it can act as the crescendo or last rising instrumental statement, signaling the finale of a vocal verse.

Notes

MIXING

IF YOU DO NOT ALREADY **have a mixing board in your production setup, I strongly suggest that you invest in one, as soon as possible. I have a Mackie™ 1604 VLZ Pro 16 Channel Mixing Board. It's about $900, but in my opinion, it beats out a number of mixers that are in a much higher price range and class! (But you can always get a used Mackie at a great price).**

Check it out. Hip Hop-Rap producers have a self-sustainable character. Often, we are completely non-dependent. We sample, chop and program all of our own music. So, I believe that we should learn to mix, or at least assist in the mix, of our own music. **(ALL of the production pioneers can, and often do, mix their own music).**

There are many advantages to having a professional mixing board within your production setup, even if it's a simple 8 channel mixing console. It allows you to take full advantage of the 8 direct outputs of the Akai S950 (or any other unit that has multiple direct outputs). By being able to isolate and mix each sound, you are able to learn more about how sounds "blend" and mix together. This in turn helps you with all future sampling, because it trains your sampling style. You become accustomed to how different sounds will play, when they're matched against each other.

Another advantage of having a professional mixing board within your production setup is that it familiarizes you with the professional mixing process. It allows you to develop your own mix sound, which is paramount to your over all production sound. Your mix training at your personal production area will translate and carry over to mix sessions at professional (commercial) recording studios.

Here, I want to point out again, that, the aim for a producer should be to develop their own quality sound. When this is achieved, the chances of a producer earning a living from their production services are dramatically increased. One thing that I tell producers, especially mid-level producers, is that **you should concentrate more on your own sound development, in particular, your drums, rather than concentrating on sounding like any of the already established producers!** Of course everybody checks out what the more established producers are doing, even the more established producers. But at some point, you have to stop mentioning or thinking about them, in relation to your own production sound, or you'll wind up either becoming a disciple of them or just a good "knock off" of what they do! That being said, you should plan on spending at least *some significant amount of time* at a professional recording studio. If you have a really professionally outfitted, home recording studio, that's cool. Just remember,

Notes

_____

_____

_____

_____

_____

_____

_____

_____

_____

_____

_____

_____

_____

_____

however, as your professional career as a producer develops, commercial recording studios are where you will be spending most of your time, not your home recording studio! (Unless of course you become REALLY established, then artists may yield to your studio choice). Either way, the point is that *you do not ever want to come off as a production vet, who's a rookie in a commercial recording studio environment!*

Again, there's nothing wrong with a maxed-out home recording studio. But the reality is, as you secure professional projects, the recording and tracking will primarily take place at larger, more professional and more better equipped recording studios. So, I would recommend using extra money for studio time, rather than *unneeded* and/or expensive gear and equipment additions. Understand, when an unknown or up-and-coming producer sells a beat, background, remix, etc. to an established artist, label and the like, the established artist is not coming to that home producer's home studio to track and record. On the contrary, this established artist will book a session at a well known studio, more often than not, a studio that they are already comfortable and familiar with. In some cases though, they'll ask for that producer's input... But this input will be in regards to other well known commercial recording studios. even the studio of that producer's choice. So, I suggest that you get familiar with the process of booking and managing recording sessions at professional recording studios that do business commercially.

MIXING APPLIED

DRUMS pt. 2

First, let me say this: **COMPRESSION IS OVER RATED**. It is the most typical stunt used in tweaking drums that I know of. So many producers think that the key to good drums is clever compression. I disagree. I believe that **the key to good drums is proper filtering, limited processing (especially limited compression) and well managed "tucking"**. Simply put, tucking is down-leveling. It's the process of fitting in or tucking a sound under other sounds in the mix. Historically, kicks and snares were the number one sounds to be tucked. However, nowadays, snares are often over compressed and "volumed out", while kicks are still tucked, but to a lesser degree. The results are beats with these

Notes

supposedly cool snares, that rip, tear and dominate, and flat kicks that punch out far too much. Overall, today's beats sound louder. But loudness, taken by itself, does not guarantee a quality sound.

If you do a good job filtering your drums, especially your kicks and snares, you will avoid a lot of mixing problems. You will also avoid having to use a lot of compression processing. (But keep in mind, sometimes compression is *needed*). Also, effective use of reverb is always a good idea. More importantly, artful **tucking** will give your drum sounds a more natural feel and far superior sound than extra compression processing. Having your own mixing board will train you in this area.

Notes

PRACTICE:
The Absolute Must

"How you practice will directly determine how successful you will be as a producer. If you're a beginning producer, you should 'leave the world' for some time. That is, cut out all things from your normal routine. If you like to hang out. Give it up for at least 3 months. Cut out any and everything that is not an absolute necessity in your life. Practice is determined by discipline, control and focus."

To PRACTICE CONSISTENTLY AND EFFECTIVELY, you have to maintain an organized, professional, and comfortable practice area. When developing your practice area, I suggest that you emulate, as much as possible, a room from a professional recording studio. STAY AWAY FROM "ALBUM WALLPAPER" and magazine cutouts. For one thing, it's not as motivating as people falsely believe. Surrounding yourself with photos of the artists and producers that you most admire will only remind you of the achievements that *they* have made. Also, it's not professional. Even though you may like it, chances are potential artists won't. Remember, a well-organized and professionally looking home studio can also double as a meeting place for potential M.C.s and other prospective Music Business contacts.

Special Note to the above point.

There was this one very well known studio in New York that recently closed. It had graffiti-laced walls and such, a real "grimey", basement feel to it. That was cool for some artists and producers, but I've spoken to a number of artists, producers and engineers who really didn't prefer working there… Among their reasons, they all mentioned that they never really liked the "feel" and "look" of the place!

Once you've got your practice area organized and situated, you should devise and map out key areas for your practice. These should be areas that you consider vital to making beats and music. They should be areas that you consider to be strong in and areas that you feel that you have deficiencies in. After you've mapped out areas for practice, divide your practice into three kinds of sessions:

MusicStudy™, BeatMaking, and Sample Disk Sessions.

Notes

MusicStudy™

The one key area of practice that I feel is absolutely the most vital to every producer's development is MusicStudy™. Before you can even begin to understand the whole craft of making quality Hip Hop-Rap Beats, you must first develop a respectable knowledge and appreciation of music and music history. Whether you favor Soul, like I do, or late 80s Hip Hop-Rap, you have to possess a respectable knowledge of music in general. That is, you have to become familiar with the basic kinds and forms of music. The three genres of music that I suggest you immediately get familiar with (if you already haven't) are: **Blues, Jazz and Soul**[1].

The Blues is the basis for all contemporary popular American Music. Musicians and singers from Sam Cooke to Jimi Hendrix trace their background to Blues Music. Even the "original" heavy metal band, Led Zepplin, trace their roots back to the Blues.

Once described as an "up-tempo" version of the Blues, **Jazz** developed and emerged as an ultimate American Art form. Through a steady stream of styles, brought on by a relentless number of talented musicians, it became one of the most transcending and influential musical disciplines in the world… (Much like how Hip Hop-Rap is today).

Soul, the culmination of the Blues, Jazz, and emerging Black Awareness, erupted into the American culture. Some of the components of Soul, like authentic social commentary, slang-based vocals, and deep grooves, became the model for some of the best Hip Hop-Rap Music ever recorded.

Familiarizing yourself with the Blues, Jazz and Soul will increase your appreciation for and improve your knowledge of music history. It will also enhance your overall grasp of contemporary music. This in turn will undoubtedly make you a better producer.

BeatTip™

Take a one-month sabbatical away from contemporary music. Block out the radio (if you haven't already). Don't watch music videos, don't listen to

---

[1] For list of artists to check out from these and other genres of music, see the MusicStudy™ Extended section.

Notes

your heavy rotation CD, just take a break from all of that. Then visit a music store that sells old or used vinyl records. Your best shot is probably a used record store. In New York, they're all over, you just gotta' "dig" for them. When you find one of these stores, go in as a student. That is, literally introduce yourself as a student who's doing a project on the history of the Blues, Jazz and Soul. Now, you should understand. The people who work in used record stores usually have a very good general knowledge of many different kinds of music. More often than not, they are especially schooled in one particular field. But I've found that no matter how broad their general knowledge of music is, *they all have a respectable knowledge of the Blues, Jazz and Soul.*

Another common characteristic of the people who work in used record stores is: they enjoy talkin' music… Even more, they enjoy sharing their musical knowledge with interested listeners. Once you ask them for some extended help, be prepared. They may offer up names and years rapidly. So, be patient and remind them that you just need a few "introductory" records to get started with. They'll hook you up… And check this out: most used vinyl record stores aren't really in it for the money. Also, many usually stock a large number of duplicate records. So, chances are you'll get a few free records with your first and future purchases.

After you get your records, set aside at least one full practice session a week for MusicStudy™. Dedicate that session to listening to music from at least one of the three main musical genres. After you've familiarized yourself with each one of these forms of music, start taking detailed notes. When you move from one sound to the next, you will naturally begin to draw comparisons.

Write those comparisons down…

For example:
- In a typical Blues song, how many bars[2] do you hear before the first change?
- Are there frequent melody changes in Blues?
- How does vocal phrasing in the Blues sound as compared to Soul?

- In Jazz, how significant is the drummer's timing?
- Is the bass thick or somewhat flat? What happens to the drums during a bass solo?
- Are there frequent melody changes in Jazz?

---

[2] A bar is one distinct musical phrase. It is a complete measure that can evenly be divided by 4 equal parts. (This simple understanding is essential to comprehending basic 4/4 timing). A bar can be composed of music alone, as is the case with most Jazz; or can be composed of lyrics alone. It also can be made up of both music and lyrics.

Notes

_____

_____

_____

_____

_____

_____

_____

_____

_____

_____

_____

_____

_____

- In Soul, what role does the one-bar loop play?
- Does Soul sound more rooted in Jazz or Blues?
- Why are the lyrics in Soul songs so urgent and real?

Making very meticulous comparisons like these, and then writing your findings down, will give you *an advantage that 9 out of 10 producers will never have.*

Once you have a respectable understanding of Blues, Jazz and Soul, continue to have regular MusicStudy™ practice sessions. However, *you must include music from other genres, as well.* Remember to also take notes on the comparisons that you make. After your one-month sabbatical from the contemporary music scene, go back—slowly! Then ask yourself, "How well does the current music scene hold up against music from the past 30 to 50 years?"

Consider this: there are entire libraries and museums that are named after and devoted to the study of musicians and singers, such as, Louis Armstrong, Bo Didley and Duke Ellington (the best composer America ever produced)... Artists and groups such as Curtis Mayfield, Aretha Franklin, Donny Hathaway, The Delfonics, and The O'Jays were inspiration for each other. And they will continue to be inspiration for those producers and recording artists that have an aim for that kind of quality music.

Note.

I'm not saying that all good music is behind us. Nor am I advocating that anyone should be stuck in the past. My point is that, music is a continuum. That is, it's a continuing process. It's a revolving, recyclable program, where quality is found again and again, through a sincere study and appreciation for the music that came before. The neglect, or in some cases, the lack of respect for the music and level of quality that came before, is in many ways, responsible for the "sound-a-like" trend in contemporary Hip Hop-Rap music.

LOOP PRACTICE

BeatTip™

Another important area of practice that I recommend that you work on, as much as possible, is the art of Looping. I use to, and from time to time, still

Notes

practice this. Set aside time for practicing and developing your loop technique. Practice looping all kinds of samples. Practice manipulating endpoints and tempos. Use both Complete Phrases™ and SparePart Phrases™. Discover what happens when you program loops to begin on the down-beat vs. the up-beat. Get to the point where you can cleanly loop everything you sample within three minutes. Understanding loop patterns and how they work with your drum programs is essential to developing and creating your own sound.

PRACTICE CHOPPING, ESPECIALLY KICKS!

If you're not good at chopping sounds, you should definitely practice sampling and chopping drum kicks. I used to do that. At one point I had about 75 drum kicks (you really only need about 5), but I used to try them ALL out in different sequences just to see how well they were chopped. This in turn helped me to root out a lot of similar sounding, unnecessary kicks. It also really helped my timing and my mixing technique. **I call kicks "bottom drivers"™, because they're responsible for driving or carrying the rhythm section and the entire beat itself.**

Note.

The above are only a few areas of practice that I isolate. But the main point is that, wherever you feel that you have a deficiency, you should isolate that area and practice it until you feel confident.

Scheduling Practice Time

The best practice is regular practice. It doesn't "really" matter how long each practice is. But it is very important to maintain a **consistent practice schedule**. In fact, I recommend that you make and rigorously follow a regular, and realistic practice schedule. Devote at least 2 to 4 hours a day, at least 3 days a week. If you can't commit to that, then at least 30 minutes a day, at least 5 days a week. Everyone has responsibilities outside of music production, so it is absolutely essential that you determine what time of the day or night is best for you. I practice late at night, usually from 11:00 p.m. to 6:00 a.m. For most people, the daytime is occupied, so it makes practicing at night almost like a default. I prefer late night practice sessions, because I feel like I'm better able to isolate my concentration. Also, professional recording sessions, involving established artists, typically run way into the early A.M. So, my practice schedule gives me an advantage. But whatever time you choose to practice, stick to it. Be sure to

Notes

_____

_____

_____

_____

_____

_____

_____

_____

_____

_____

_____

_____

_____

_____

"clearly" let your family and close friends know your schedule. Because It is absolutely paramount that they know and respect your schedule.

BeatTip™

ESTABLISH CONSISTENT, REALISTIC PRACTICE GOALS

Be honest about your level of production, then begin improving it. Determine how much you wanna' improve your level daily, weekly and monthly. Once you can feel and hear that your level of production has improved, devise a direction for where you want to go in your daily, weekly and monthly practice sessions. For every time you practice, aside from MusicStudy™ and area-aimed practicing, produce at least one beat! Every week, produce at least 5 beats. Every month, produce at least 15 beats. Have your own battle of the beats with those 15 beats. The beats that lose, go straight to the garbage. A lot of producers will stress that you should never throw a beat away. I strongly disagree. Every producer has compared their production to that of established producers. And it's always clear how close or far off you are. If you make a beat and the quality of your production is too far off from where you're trying to be, dump the beat in the garbage. If it's whack, but there's still something about the beat, well then keep it. But the more self-admitting whack beats that you keep, the slower the development of your production level will be... **MAINTAIN QUALITY CONTROL EVERY 2 WEEKS!**

Now, the top 5 beats that win your personal beat battles, should tell you what your sound is, or at least where it's going. These are the beats that you want to keep and study. Your goal should be to produce at that level or better every month.

Down-time Management

When your're not practicing, you should be practicing. That is, in your down-time away from your setup, there are a number of ways to continually improve yourself as a producer, including reading, organizing your practice notes, etc.

Notes

Catalogue your development

Write down what you've improved on or struggled with each month. If you felt that you made a major leap in the level of your production, write it down. If you preview your beats for M.C.s and other people, write down the responses that you've gotten from that month's beats.

MUSIC BOOKS AND/OR MUSIC FILMS AND DOCUMENTARIES

Read the biographies of acclaimed Musicians, Singers, Producers and other Entertainers. Reading about the lives, the trials and triumphs of these people will give you a good indication of what it takes to make it. Also, you will be able to more adequately gauge the stages of your own career and development. One of the best music books that I ever read was "Bob Marley", by Stephen Davis, published by Schenkman Books. My favorite music film, "The Harder They Come", starring Jimmy Cliff, was actually not a documentary at all. But the grit and the underlying music theme is undeniably relevant to any artist or musician who's ever believed in their sound and abilities.

Notes

_____

_____

_____

_____

_____

_____

_____

_____

_____

_____

_____

_____

_____

ADVANCED PRODUCERS

Notes

MusicStudy™ EXTENDED

MUSIC PRODUCTION THEORY

Studying music is absolutely critical to the overall development of a Hip Hop-Rap producer. An understanding of the various music production theories is key to every producers development. In Hip Hop-Rap there are three main production theories: **Samples Featured Production**; **No Samples Featured Production**; and **Samples Featured with Instrumentation Production**. I consider them as three separate schools of thought.

Samples Featured Production relies primarily on the use of record samples. Usually, producers of this school of thought, try to remain close to the vain of the golden era of Hip Hop-Rap production: 1988-1995. In fact, the most noticeable characteristic of this style of production is its timeless sound. The theory frowns upon "lazy", unimaginative keyboard beats and the like. However, the **Samples Featured Production** does leave room for useful keyboard phrases, percussion, etc. But for the most part, this theory is built on sampling records, for every needed sound. Also, this production style often produces a sound, reminiscent to that aforementioned golden era of Hip Hop-Rap. Usually, Producers from this school of thought are masters at Sample Editing, especially chopping and looping. And they tend to almost always exclusively use classic production setups (i.e., Akai S950, Akai MPC 60(II), E-Mu SP 1200, Ensoniq ASR 10).

No Samples Featured Production relies heavily upon the use of keyboards and/or sound modules. Although some of this production is of quality, I find that it usually lacks a real soul *"feeling"*. *The most ironic thing about this theory is that, samples are actually being used!* Whether a sample comes from records or sound cartridges (full of sampled sounds), or sample disks, WAV files, etc., *its still a sample*. Unfortunately, I've often found that the practitioners of this theory are more concerned with making it known that they use no samples, than they are with making quality beats and music. Typically, producers from this school of thought view Sampled Featured Production as too limiting and often inferior. In fact, they often like to view themselves as "complete" producers; and in some cases, even as musicians. Producers from this production school of thought tend to almost always exclusively use contemporary production setups (i.e., Akai MPC 2000XL, Korg Triton).

The **Samples Featured with Instrumentation Production theory** is a cross between the two previously mentioned theories. Not quite as rigidly focused on exclusively using record samples, like Samples Featured Production; and yet not as interdependent upon

Notes

keyboards and/or sound modules, as with No Samples Featured Production, Samples Featured with Instrumentation Production is perhaps the most ambitious and rewarding of all the three theories. The central aim of this production theory is to achieve the right blend of record samples, keyboards and/or sound modules. In some cases, producers from this school of thought will make beats that only feature record samples. And in some cases, they will produce beats that only feature keyboards and sound modules. However, in most cases, their beats are composed of a combination of record samples, keyboards and/or sound modules. Producers from this school of thought usually tend to either use classic production setups or a combination of classic and contemporary setups (i.e. Akai MPC 60II, Akai MPC 3000, Korg Triton, Akai S950, Roland XP 80).

Samples Featured with Instrumentation Production is the most prominently held production theory. It clearly offers the most possibilities. Ironically, however, it contributes to the least interesting, least soul sounding production. The reason being: because **too many producers "over-gear"**™. What I mean is that **they often obtain and use unnecessary gear, within their production**. The general rule is that the more gear and equipment that you have in your production setup, the harder it will be to master your setup! Far too regularly, producers "add" something to a beat that isn't needed. Sometimes this is because they maintain a perfection level that is too impractical. But a lot of times, it's because they insist on using *every* piece of gear within their setup. If you have two main pieces of gear and equipment, i.e., a sampler and a sequencer, obviously it must always be used. But when you have multiple samplers, multiple keyboards, multiple sound modules, and multiple effects processors (by the way, I do not recommend too many effects processors in small home pre-production studios), it is NEVER necessary to use all, for the purpose of composing one Hip Hop-Rap beat!

Though the Sample Featured with Instrumentation Production theory does offer a lot more production possibilities, I find that the Samples Featured Production theory offers the fastest opportunity for setup mastery. Contrary to a somewhat widely held belief, that sampling records limits your production capabilities, I believe that sampling records is limitless; depending of course on your sampling style, or rather, "how" you sample and what types of samples that you like to use in your production. I also strongly believe that it opens up a very unique opportunity for Hip Hop-Rap production. When you sample a record, you are sampling an era, a mood, a feeling. This in turn allows you to interpolate or translate that era, mood and/or feeling into the present, while

Notes

shaping the mood and feeling, accordingly. In fact, I believe that sampling records provides you with a better ability to produce a sound that is as much current, as it is "timeless".

I do not particularly favor the **No Samples Featured Production theory.** The main reason is because the majority of the producers, who claim no samples, usually have very little musical understanding and/or no training with ANY instrument, let alone the keyboard or drums. Therefore, the results are bubble-gum, clown-like beats, that are often unimaginative and lazy. Moreover, the sounds and styles of these beats are often copied, and not even re-worked to cover the obvious biting. However, there are some producers from this school of production who actually have had training with the piano or other instruments. As it follows, they also have a vast musical knowledge and background. In these rare cases, the beats are high quality! Unfortunately, the number of high-quality No Samples Featured Production producers is small.

Notes

PRODUCERS and/or RECORDING ARTISTS OF SPECIAL NOTE

Among The countless number of musicians, singers, bands and song writers who are worthy of a very committed study, I feel that there are14 producers and/or recording artists, in particular, that all Hip Hop-Rap producers should study real closely. They are: **Curtis Mayfield, Bob Marley, Aretha Franklin, James Brown, Kenneth Gamble and Leon Huff (Gamble and Huff), Donny Hathaway, King Tubby, Tina Marie, Quincy Jones, Led Zepplin, Stevie Wonder, Albert King, John Coltrane** and **Marvin Gaye.**

Curtis Mayfield

One of the original members of the excellent group, The Impressions, Curtis Mayfield went solo a couple of years after the group's lead singer, Jerry Butler, left to pursue his own solo career. Among his great catalogue of albums, I would say "Superfly" is the most quintessential; start with this album! Curtis Mayfield wrote, produced, composed arranged and performed all of his own music. He was also a pioneer, in that he was one of the first blacks to record for his *own* record label (Curtom Records).

Bob Marley and The Wailers

Contrary to popular belief, Bob Marley, the leader of The Wailin' Wailers (the Original name of the group), was not simply a great Reggae singer. He was a Jamaican Soul singer. He openly admitted how much he was influenced by American Soul Music, in particular, **Curtis Mayfield**. In fact, a great deal of the Wailers' earlier songs, were Curtis Mayfield and Impressions' covers. Among the Wailers' huge catalogue of classic music, I recommend beginning with "Burnin".

Aretha Franklin

I'm impressed most by Aretha Franklin's vocal range. And I'm not talking about high and low pitch, I'm talking about song and material capability. Aretha Franklin's ability to sing the Blues, Jazz, and Soul, all with the same aggressive, wit, pallet and attention, will never be matched. She wrote, arranged and produced a great deal of her own material, in an era where women (especially

Notes

black women) were often not allowed to even have a say. But whether she wrote the song or not, you could be sure of one thing: an Aretha Franklin song was always sincere, aggressive, soft, and magnificently styled. Among the many tremendous songs within her catalogue of music, I recommend starting with "Young, Gifted and Black".

James Brown

I call him "the Pioneer". In my opinion, James Brown's ability to blend entertainment with solid, straight-at-you social commentary, was his greatest legacy. His music, which was strictly soulful, featured deceptively simple patterns and phrases, had the biggest influence on Hip Hop-Rap Music Production. I really can't single out one James Brown song or album. Anything from '69 to '75 deserves a very close study.

Kenneth Gamble and Leon Huff- Gamble & Huff (producers)

In my opinion, there will never be a better production team than Gamble & Huff! Their sound was the most controlled, distinctive, gimmick-free thing that I ever heard. When they produced for an artist, they didn't just rent out their sound, like today's prominent Hip Hop-Rap production teams. On the contrary, Gamble & Huff gave an artist their sound and asked that artist to simply enhance it. I suggest that you start with one of the O'Jays' earlier albums. Then check out The Jacksons' self-titled 1976 release. Most Soul Music historians credit Quincy Jones as the biggest production influence on Michael Jackson (ca. 1979-1985). However, it is my contention that NO ONE influenced Michael Jackson as much as Gamble & Huff did. Even though they were the residential producers for the mighty Philadelphia International Records imprint, both Gamble and Huff established their own separate recording labels.

Donny Hathaway

Donny Hathaway carried the dignity of the black ghetto inside of his urgent, unrelenting and incredibly warm, soulful sound. Like **Bob Marley**, he was a student of **Curtis Mayfield**. In fact, early on he trained under and played with Curtis Mayfield; no doubt gaining the seeds for his very melodic musical arrangements. (In fact, as a teenager, Donny Hathaway was a member of the Curtis Mayfield created and produced group, *The Mayfield Singers*). Of all the songs that I've ever heard, from any artist from any era, Donny Hathaway's recording of **"Someday We'll All Be Free"**, is my favorite. I recommend you start there.

Notes

King Tubby

The undisputed "king" of Dub Music was the infamous King Tubby. An electrician and engineer by trade, the Jamaican, King Tubby, designed and crafted his own mixing console and went on to be one of the definers of the "Jamaican sound", particularly, 70s Dub. He influenced everyone from **Bob Marley** to **The English Beat**. But his influence on Kool Herc, is what Hip Hop-Rap producers should be concerned with! King Tubby has way too much too mention. You can start anywhere with King Tubby.

Tina Marie

Tina Marie was one of the most creatively interesting and soulful songwriters of all time. She wrote her own music and lyrics, and played multiple instruments. She also produced and arranged nearly all of her own material. Like **Aretha Franklin**, Tina Marie had a masterful range. What I find particularly interesting about her is how she sang over or above her music, seemingly off the beat, but in reality, right on. I recommend starting with "It Must Be magic". This is one of my top five favorite albums, of any artist, any era, any style.

Quincy Jones

Quincy Jones is a very good model for modern producers. His production and arrangements carried an incredible range. From Blues to Jazz to Soul and back... Quincy Jones' music graced a countless number of albums, as well a large number of motion pictures (one of my favorite film scores of all time, "They Called Me Mister Tibbs", was done by Quincy Jones). I also remember reading liner notes from one of his albums, where he discussed his desire to someday develop a television show. You will not go wrong listening to anything that Quincy Jones has produced.

Led Zepplin

No rock group was heavier than Led Zepplin. Their music was very uniquely underscored by the Blues. Rock bass often sounds flat, and tucked entirely too much... Not Led Zepplin. Their bass banged, and their drums kicked! I recommend checking out their first four albums (I through IV), in chronological order.

Stevie Wonder

Like **Curtis Mayfield**, **James Brown** and **Bob Marley**, Stevie Wonder's music (late 60s to late 70s) was a terrific blend of soul and social commentary. Not only a great singer/songwriter, he played multiple instruments. His support for and heavy use of electronic keyboards and synthesizers helped propel the creation

Notes

of various electronic instruments and devices, most notably, digital samplers. There are two Stevie Wonder albums that I think everyone should have (regardless if you are a producer or not): "Innervisions" and "Songs in the Key of Life".

Marvin Gaye

I never understood why Marvin Gaye's vocal timing was so accurate until I found out that he was a trained drummer. In fact, he was an excellent sessions drummer, often playing on a number of the earlier Motown hits. As it follows, the genius of Marvin Gaye lied in his rhythm. One of the most recognizable advocates of soul music, Marvin Gaye always represented the blunt realities of common society. I suggest starting with the album, "Let's Get It On".

John Coltrane

Of all the jazz musicians that I've heard before, I relate most to John Coltrane. He played the tenor sax at one speed: hard. But even still, there was a unique, non-offending tone to his hardness. In fact, the blues that underscored his music was as much aggressive as it was surprisingly subtle. You can study anything from John Coltrane. From his time with the first Miles Davis Quintet, up until his creation of "A Love Surpreme", you can not go wrong studying anything from John Coltrane.

Albert King

Like all Blues Music, Albert King's Blues was deeply rooted in the common, everyday struggle and hustle. However, unlike all Blues Music, Albert King's Blues had an extremely soulful appeal. I recommend starting with "I'll Play The Blues For You".

Notes

HIP HOP- RAP PRODUCERS AND/OR ARTISTS THAT SHOULD BE STUDIED

Eric B. & Rakim (Golden Era Pioneers)

First study the album, "Paid in Full".

If ALL of Hip Hop-Rap was taken away from me, and I had the chance to get one thing back, it would be the song "Paid in Full". On this verse alone, Rakim set a lyrical bar that has only been since matched by two other M.C.s!

Marley Marl (Golden Era Pioneer)

First study the song, "The Symphony"

Could anybody flip the signature samples like Marley Marl?

Marley Marl figured out "something" about production and sampling, way before anybody else did. No one else is as responsible for pioneering the sampling movement as much as Marley Marl, word up.

Kool G Rap & DJ Polo (Golden Era Pioneers)

First study the song, "Road to the Riches"

"...I was sort of a porter, takin' the next man's order."

The only way you write a line like that is if you're feeling the beat, word up. Like Rakim, Kool G. Rap could talk street "authentically". But more important than that was the fact that Kool G Rap was extremely articulate, and very rhythm responsive… Moreover, unknown to most, Kool G. Rap was very politically informed!

Slick Rick the Ruler (Golden Era Pioneer)

Study the album, "The Great Adventures of Slick Rick the Ruler"

One of the most widely unknown facts was that Slick Rick actually produced a lot of his own music. All storytellers study Slick Rick the Ruler.

Notes

Gang Starr (Golden Era/Modern Era Pioneers)

First study the album, "Daily Operation"; followed by DJ Premier's first production for M.O.P. Gang Starr is an excellent study in consistency. They are also an example of how to succeed without compromising your integrity. No other group, duo, or solo artist in the history of Hip Hop-Rap have been able to remain as uncorrupted, and uncompromising, for as long as Gang Starr has.

The RZA (Golden Era/Modern Era Pioneer)

First study the song "Cakes" (off of the Ghost Dog Motion Picture Soundtrack), rather than Wu Tang's "36 Chambers". Then work your way backwards through his discography! The RZA was the first to incorporate and feature sped-up soul vocal samples. He was also the first producer that I ever heard stress the importance of mixing your own production.

Boogie Down Productions (BDP-KRS ONE) (Golden Era Pioneer)

First study the song, "Love's Gonna' Get You", then study "The P Is Still Free". Despite KRS-ONE'S well known moniker, "The Teacher", which is associated with his social and political consciousness, these two songs let you know exactly why the streets listened to and respected KRS-ONE and the BDP Massive!
Yo, the first show I ever saw was KRS ONE, up at The Fever, in the Bronx… I went with this beautiful, fox, who eventually became the mother of my son…

Public Enemy (Golden Era Pioneer)

First study the album, "Yo, Bum Rush the Show"
One of the best studies in unique, authentic sound.
P.E. made political and social commentary sound good, not out-of-touch or overworked. The most unique thing about Chuck D, who is always overlooked and left off top 5, and top 10 lists, is the fact that his rhyme style was just extension of his oratorical skills.

Mobb Deep (Late Golden Era/Modern Era Pioneers)

First study the album, "The Infamous".
This is one of the best Hip Hop-Rap albums ever assembled!
"Shook Ones" pt. 2 is proof that you don't have to make a club banger to have a club banger!

Notes

M.C. Lyte (Golden Era Pioneer)

First study the song, "Paper Thin".

One of my top 5 M.C.s, period… And I'm not talkin' about females, nahmean… I'm talkin' of ALL M.C.s!

Truth be told: a lot of critically acclaimed rappers (ALL male) bit HEAVILY from M.C. Lyte…

LL Cool J (Golden Era Pioneer)

Study the album, "My Radio"

Here's somethin' that's not widely known:

LL from this album, this era… would've roasted anybody in a battle.

The Wu-Tang Clan (Mid Golden Era Pioneers)

Study the album, "Enter the Wu-Tang (36 Chambers)"

Respect this album for the music, but also respect this album because it was one of the first to strike a blow in the fight for the Hip Hop-Rap Industry.

Queen Latifah (Golden Era Pioneer)

First study the song, "Dance for Me"

Mark the 45 King and early Queen Latifah, nahmean…

Again, another female in my top 10 list. She rhymed with more heart and aggressiveness than many of the "so-called" thugs and gangsters that are out, posturing right now, word up.

Ghostface Killah (Mid Golden Era/Modern Era Pioneer)

Study the album, "Supreme Clientele"

This album is a classic, plain n' simple. I've never heard a better managed Hip Hop-Rap album… Every beat was chosen carefully… Moreover, the song arrangement for this album has still yet to be matched.

Main Source (The Large Professor… Golden Era Pioneer)

Study the album, "Breaking Atoms"

If you do not have this album, get it! This album prompted a lot of people to start producing.

Pete Rock & CL Smooth (Golden Era Pioneers)

First study the song, "Straighten It Out"

Could've mentioned nearly anything, but this song signaled a change in Pete Rock's sound.

Notes

Nas (Mid Golden Era/Modern Pioneer)

Study the album, "Illmatic"

A rare achievement that, ironically, continued and ended some of what was good about Hip Hop-Rap. This album featured production by three of the most critically acclaimed Hip Hop-Rap pioneers... Two of three were in their prime when this album was released. However, one of the three developed even further.

NWA (Golden Era Pioneers)

First study the song, "Straight Outta' Compton"

NWA made it possible to rep from any hood. Way too much attention is paid to what they did for West Coast/Gangsta Rap. NOT ENOUGH ATTENTION PAID TO WHAT THEY DID FOR RAP!

Screwball

Study the album, "Y2K: The Album"

This is the most slept on Hip Hop-Rap album of all time.

Production was very well managed throughout the entire album.

RUN DMC (Golden Era Pioneers)

First study the song, "It's Like That", then study the album, "Raising Hell"

This is one of the most brilliantly put together albums ever. All too often it's easy to forget how good Run DMC was. Indeed, we all often mention their name out of respect and such, but a real study would reveal how mean RUN DMC really was... From timing, to delivery, to flow, to production... they put it down.

Diamon D

Study the album, "Stunts, Blunts & Hip Hop"

Solid production, consistent sound.

M.O.P. (Mid Golden Era Pioneers/Modern Pioneers)

First study the song "How About Some Hardcore".

M.O.P is volume 10+. Their translation of hood to music is ALL authentic.

I hear Brooklyn first, music second when I listen to M.O.P... That's what I like about them. And DON'T nobody STOMP OUT a beat like M.O.P...

Notes

The Notorious B.I.G.
(Biggie Smalls{Mid Golden Era Pioneer})
Study the album, "Ready to Die"
The range of production on this album offers a very good study in production management.

The Neptunes (Modern Era Pioneers)
First study "Superthug", then "Hot Damn"
Often emulated but never duplicated. The Neptunes, contrary to jealous belief, don't just pump out hits. These cats know music. They know instrumentation and music history, very well.
(And from what I hear, neither the Korg Triton, nor the MPC 2000XL, are their production weapons of choice).

The Beatnuts
First study the song "The Reign of the Tek"
Consistent production.

Showbiz & AG
Study the album, "Runaway Slave"
Yo, Showbiz flipped and tried a lot things that a number producers still can't figure out. Study this album and learn somethin' about structuring bars.

Big Daddy Kane
Study the album, "Long Live the Kane"
This album showed how far the signature samples could be taken.

O.C.
Study the album, "Word...Life"
The album is warm and consistent throughout.

Jay Z (Golden Era/Modern Era Pioneer)
First study the song, "Feelin' It", then study the song "Girls, Girls, Girls"
Notice the crossroads between early Jay Z and the Jay Z we know, now. Say ANYTHING you want to about Jay Z... what he represents, what "you think" you know his motives are. But at the end of the day, I dare you to say Jay Z ain't nice!

Notes

Dr. Dre (Golden Era/Modern Era Pioneer)

Study the album, "The Chronic"

Dr. Dre's music is like a classic arrangement. His production is always managed well, never over-produced.

The Beastie Boys (Golden Era/Modern Era Pioneers)

Study the album, "Paul's Boutique"

This album signaled that the Beastie Boys would be returning to their instrumental roots.

A Tribe Called Quest (Mid Golden Era Pioneers)

First study the song, "Steve Biko"

Many producers study A Tribe Called Quest for their snares. However, on this song, you wanna' study how the bass was filtered.

Tupac (Mid Golden Era Pioneer)

First study the song, "You Are Appreciated"

The appeal of Tupac was that he said it straight and plain, while never forcing or competing with the mood of the beat.

Kanye West (Modern Era Pioneer)

First study the song, "Get By"

In my opinion, this is Kanye West's best production.

Buckwild

First study the song, "Time's Up"

This song gives you the first sign of his production range.

Biz Markie

First study the song, "The Vapors"

Like Marley Marl, Biz Markie figured out early on how the signature samples could effectively be manipulated.

Notes

MARKETING and PROMOTING YOUR PRODUCTION

Building a Beat and Music Catalogue

CATALOGUING YOUR BEATS AND MUSIC is essential. Whether you give your beats and music names or assign them numbers, as I do, maintaining an organized record of what you produce is critical. Nearly every producer who has reached some level of production expertise has produced a music demo for someone. It doesn't matter if it was a local M.C. or an established artist, the point is, once created, the production *is* your catalogue. The easiest way to build a catalogue is to produce as many demos as you possibly can. There are a countless number of nice M.C.s, who unfortunately, have no access to original beats and music. Indeed, a lot of them are regulated to honing their rhyme skills to the instrumentals of popular songs, that usually do not fit their developing styles.

BeatTip™

Given the opportunity, these "undiscovered", or rather, not well-known M.C.s, would gladly write to original material. So, rather than "sit" on your beats and music, locate these motivated M.C.s and offer your production services on a full credit basis. That is, offer to construct their demo for full production credit and non-pay. (Remember, an artist demo produced by you is also *your* demo). If you're in a position to cover studio costs, you should do so. If not, stipulate that the artist pays for all studio time, or split the cost of studio time! Of course, you should receive some financial compensation for your time and direction. The best way to achieve this is to stipulate that the artist must pay for all associated accessory costs, like CDs, floppy disks, DATs, etc.

I also recommend preparing an invoice and a simple contract; or at least some simple agreement in writing. The invoice should be a dated record of which beats and music and services that you provided, along with the name of the artist(s) that received those services. Quicken 2003 Premier Home & Business is an excellent software program that quickly and easily allows you to create and

Notes

customize these kinds of invoices. It's only about $55 and it's well worth it. You will also want to have a written agreement between you and the artist(s) that you provide your production services for. If you're not familiar with drafting a production agreement, don't worry. Just remember to include three things in your agreement: 1. the name(s) of all parties involved; 2. the terms, including initial and end dates, fees and penalties (if applicable), and any bonus features that you may think of. For instance, you might include in the agreement that the duration is a "one-off"; that the agreement ends once the project is completed. However, you might include a clause that stipulates: in the event that the artist(s) gains a record deal, using the beats and music provided by you/your company, the artist must pay 10% of their awarded recording budget. You might also stipulate that: in the event that the artist(s) desires to use the demo beats for a commercial release, the artist must pay a pre-determined price to you (your production company) for the beats and music. Point is, covering all expenses for promising artists not only allows you to build your beats and music catalogue, it presents you with the tremendous opportunity for potential exposure and revenue!

Creating and Incorporating Your Production Company

If you haven't already created and incorporated your production company, you should do so immediately. I know a lot of producers who have "illegitimate" or rather unincorporated production companies. This is not the way to go. Simply coming up with a nice name for a music production company will not do it. To really be legitimate, you should be incorporated and registered as a legal corporation in your city and state. There are a number advantages to incorporating your production company. Incorporation instantly transforms your company into a legal entity, making it and/or you eligible for numerous credit and financial benefits, that you will undoubtedly need. Another advantage of starting and incorporating your own production company is that It boosts your confidence and it gives you a foundation from which to build upon. It informs people that your company is a legitimate business, in good legal standing. And it helps Music Industry Insiders to identify how serious you are about your music production. In fact, record labels and the like are more inclined to do business with an incorporated company, as compared to an unincorporated one…

"If your production company is not incorporated, it is not a legal corporation. If you have not at least formed a Sole Propri-

Notes

etorship or Partnership in your local city or county municipality, then you are not legally authorized to conduct business."

Incorporating your music production company is rather easy. You do not *need* a lawyer or an accountant to incorporate your business. In fact, you can easily incorporate your business yourself. (I incorporated my business myself). Each state has rules and regulations that you must adhere to in order to successfully complete the incorporation process. However, the process is usually very simple. In New York, all you need to do is file a Certificate of Incorporation. The forms are available on the New York State Department of State website (www.dos.state.ny.us/corp/corpwww.html) and at various stationary stores. You need only to fill out the form and send it to the New York Department of State Division of Corporations. When you send in the form, you must also include the required fees. The current filing fees for a Certificate of Incorporation in the state of New York are: $125.00, plus $10.00 for a Certified Copy of the Certificate of Incorporation, you may also send an additional $25.00 for expedited handling, which I strongly recommend because it ensures that your certificate will be processed within 24 hours. Other states vary in the way that they process requests for incorporation, however, most states usually employ a process very similar to how it's done in New York.

Notes

SHOPPING YOUR BEATS AND MUSIC

BEFORE YOU BEGIN SHOPPING YOUR beats and music, you need to be honest with your level of production. If you really feel that your beats and music are ready, meaning: your production sounds *as good* (if not better) than the beats and music that is currently being heard, either commercially on the radio, OR underground in clubs and on mix tapes. If you can realistically say yes to this, then by ALL MEANS PROCEED. However, if *you're not sure* of your sound or production level, then you're probably not ready to shop your material yet. Let's assume you're ready…

To effectively shop your material, you have to give a good demonstration of what you've done and what you're capable of doing. A typical demonstration or "demo" should be at least 10 beats, no more than 30. However, whatever number of nice beats that you have is what you got! The most widely accepted format that these beats should be on is a CD or CD-R. Some producers have their demos on DATs, ADATs and even 2-inch Reels. But the problem with this is, it's simply not practical. The average person nowadays only has access to a CD player—not a DAT machine, an ADAT machine or a 2-inch reel machine.

The way that you should assemble your Demo CD is like this. First, dedicate a couple of practice sessions just for the purpose of making your Demo CD. Once you've scheduled the appropriate practice time, the first thing that you should do is gather together about 30 of your best beats. If you don't have 30 beats, don't worry, go with what you have. But you should at least have 10 or more. These must be beats that you *really* feel. If you've previewed some of them for M.C.s and other people before, that's fine—provided you got back sincere, positive feedback. (And I mean sincere feedback, not that typical: "that's hot"). Next, spend about three days having these beats battle off, until you reach your top 15. Once you've done that, you're ready to build your Beat & Music Demo.

BeatTip™

The first beat should be your third best!

A lot of producers and so-called Music Industry Insiders will tell you to put your best beat first, on a Music Demo. *But what they won't tell you is*: if

Notes

you're not an established producer, your beats will be listened to from the perspective point that you are whack! You see, music is very saturated right now. Everyone, from label execs to studio interns, knows this. So, nowadays, *if* and when most A&Rs listen to your demo, they'll *expect* to hear nothing impressive. So, they'll only check to see if there's at least one good beat. I've seen producers and A&Rs listen to the opening track of a demo, for about 15 or 20 seconds, then scan to track 3. They'll actually listen to track 3 longer than they will track 1! Remember, they've already assumed that your material is whack, but they're looking for a surprise. This is why you should lead your demo off with a 30 second snippet of your third best beat and/or song, followed by a 40 second snippet of your best beat and/or song, followed by 60 snippet of your second best beat and/or song. (Remember, if your entire catalogue is bangin', it won't matter what order your selections are in, you feel me). All songs after that should be a variation between 40 to 60 seconds. See, to most A&Rs, your second best will sound like the best, so they'll rewind to the first two tracks to see if they missed anything. Then they'll really study your demo to check for your full potential. **Remember, you're not trying to showcase the fact that you can make *one* good beat.** *You wanna' demonstrate that you are capable of making <u>multiple</u> quality beats and music, consistently, and sometimes more importantly, rapidly.*

Get your Beats & Music Demo to Established Producers first, A&Rs second.

"Your best chance for getting recognized, and thus production work, will come from either an established producer or an A&R Rep."

Producers have the unique freedom to work on multiple projects, simultaneously. A producer can be involved with as many albums or projects that he or she wants to. They are not limited by the number and/or type of projects; nor are they confined to any particular musical genre. One producer can have beats and music on three or four albums, a film soundtrack, and a television series, all at the same time! In a case like this, not only does the producer get his or her base agreed upon payment, or rather the pre-determined price of the beat, they receive additional revenue in the form of publishing, licensing, residual payments, etc. Also, a producers' base pay isn't dependent upon the success of a project. That is, producers get their base pay, upon delivery of their

Notes

production, directly from the artists' budget or some other pre-arranged agreement, whether the project is a hit or not. In fact, producers actually do business like general contractors. On the other hand, the average rapper, who all told, really only makes about $30,000.00 to $60,000.00 a year, after taxes, (and this is if everything's somewhat of a success) has to wait until their quarterly checks arrive! Do you see the producers' advantage?

Consider this:

In the Music Recording Industry, it's common knowledge that a number of well-known producers do not actually make their beats. In fact, a lot of times they have a number of "unknown" producers who create beats for them. These well-known producers, who are often in demand, then make "edits" or "changes" to the initial (original) creations. Most of the time, they make no changes at all. These well-known producers then sell the final product (beat) to a well-known recording artist. So, who gets the production credit, the publishing points and the big producer's paycheck? The well-known producer, of course!

This system has always been a part of the Music Recording Industry. In the Music Business, time is absolutely critical. **This is why some producers have other producers make or "jump-start" beats for them.** Now check out this hypothetical (but realistic) scenario: a top-level producer gets 10 project requests- that is, 10 separate artists/projects, due out over a 4 to 6 weeks time frame, all running consecutively. Understand, most Rap artists like to preview (listen) to at least 10 to 15 beats before they choose. So, let's say each artist wants to preview at least 10 beats. Is it *possible* for this top-level music producer to kick out 100 *quality* beats in this short amount of time? Sure, it is… But how difficult do you think this would be? Keep in mind, this is a top-level producer, so they were already working on other projects, before they accepted these additional 10 new ones! Get the picture? In a case like this, a top-level producer is definitely going to "farm-out" or even turnover some of the production work to his network of producers.

"Point is, if a producer feels your production, they are 100 times more likely to get you paid production work, than an A&R, or any other Music Industry Insider, for that matter."

However, some A&Rs are actually very valuable. One of the biggest myths in music, especially Hip Hop-Rap, is that artists choose their own beats. Though some artists actually do have this right, most artists have to rely on what they receive from their A&R Rep. Don't get me wrong, if you meet an artist or have a

Notes

_____

_____

_____

_____

_____

_____

_____

_____

_____

_____

_____

_____

_____

_____

connection with an established artist, it's still a good idea to get your beats and music to them. Just remember, in most cases, the A&R Rep, not the artist(s), has the final say when it comes to beat selection!

A lot of A&Rs are quick to say that they're always looking for new material. Translation: they're always looking for new material from established producers, at bargain prices. Contrary to what they are actually supposed to do, A&Rs typically DO NOT seek out unknown producers. In interviews and in the public eye, they'll often give phony-talk about how they're *always looking for new artists and new material*, when in reality, most of today's Hip Hop-Rap A&Rs are simply not motivated, nor aggressive in finding new talent OR new production material. In fact, the only time the majority of them even offer a semblance of what they are actually supposed to do is when they know that their job is on the line. Listen, the Music Business Registry (known as the A&R Registry) is the official label to label business contact source. It's published EVERY 8 WEEKS! This rapid publication isn't because there are so many great new positions be filled… On the contrary, the termination rate of Music Industry professionals, in particular, A&Rs is outrageous. But here's the most ironic thing about this: the majority of A&Rs can't seem to figure out *why* they tend to lose their jobs regularly.[1] However, all this being said, there are a handful of A&Rs and other Music Industry insiders, who actually pursue new talent and material. And if presented correctly, they *will* give some fresh material a quick listen. So, how do you submit material to the *right* A&Rs?

BeatTip™

First, make a list of at least 5 A&R Reps, who worked on projects that you felt were of quality, but maybe did not gain big commercial success. Look on the backs or inserts of CD covers of your favorite artists, and check the A&R credits… Talk to anyone that you know in the Music Recording Industry… Call Recording Studios… (The more creative you are with coming up with A&R Rep names the better). After you've got your target list together, you're ready to make moves.

---

[1] Nearly every well known Hip Hop-Rap artist in the last 10 years was initially "passed over" by *at least* 3 major labels.

Notes

The absolute best place to catch a good A&R Rep or an established producer is in the recording studio. (As I mentioned earlier in the manual, developing a relationship with well-known recording studios will pay major dividends). Send your material, via overnight express mail, to the studios where your target A&R Reps and producers have been known to frequent. Make sure you attention it to the A&R and NOT the recording studio staff. If you have a production company, it works better because the package and presentation will look more legitimate. If you don't have a company, make one up. Either way, give your contact address and numbers. Remember, all you're trying to do is get your music heard.

If it's good, you will get contacted.

You can also send your material to your target A&R's office. Just don't do a blind mailing. That is, never mail or messenger your material off to anyone or anywhere without a contact. If you know an A&R Rep personally, that's excellent. But chances are, most up-in-coming producers do not know an A&R Rep personally. So, one way to get around this involves the phone call initiative. That is, after you've properly targeted the A&Rs that you feel would be interested in your material, call their offices and speak to their *assistants*. Never ask to speak to the A&R Rep directly, unless you're confident in your talk-game. Instead, ask for the assistant of… If you know the assistant's name already, you're way ahead.

You should be straight up and ready to deal. Remember, most assistants are always looking to advance their own careers, so if you present the deal well, they'll usually go for it. The deal goes like this: Ask the assistant if you could submit your material directly to them (the assistant). Assistants usually collect and pass on all important mail, directly to the A&R Rep, anyway. More importantly, many *assistants*, and not the A&Rs whom they assist, are actually the ones that screen in-coming music demos!

All right, so check it out., when you speak to the assistant(s), tell them that you're willing to give them a 10% finder's fee (commission) if their boss likes and uses any of your beats and music that they (the assistant) passed on. In most cases, the assistant will tell you to mail your Beat CD/Demo directly to them. If you live in the same city, I recommend having it sent over via messenger, immediately after the conversation. But if you don't live in the city of your target A&R Rep, sending your Beat CD/Demo overnight express is the second best option. **If the assistant is impressed, even in the least, by your music, you've made yourself a major contact and ally.** In fact, you can keep sending the assistant(s) more and more material… Like I said, **most assistants are looking**

Notes

to move up. So, they'll try to make it happen. Even if the A&R Rep that they work for doesn't dig your music, they will actually shop it around the industry. I not only had someone A&R my first album *for free*, I had my main Beat and Music CD shopped around the industry through a former assistant, who now works as a Marketing Rep for a major label.

Notes

GETTING PAID:
Beat Prices, Contracts and Agreements

How Much Should You Charge for Your Beats and Music

The common industry standard payment range for a beat/track, (produced by an unknown or not-yet established producer), intended to be used on the commercial release of an established artist, is $2,500-$10,000. However, since price is always negotiable, this price can easily deflate or inflate.

There are many factors that go into determining how much producers should charge for their beats. **Notoriety** is perhaps the most important factor for a well-known producer. However, notoriety isn't a luxury that lesser known producers rarely get the chance to experience. On the contrary, *producers on the come-up* have to use a different set of factors, in determining how much they ultimately charge for their beats and music.

The 4 most important factors that must be considered when determining how much you should charge for your beats and music are:

1. Your judgment of your overall quality of your Production Catalogue...

Do you honestly feel that you have quality, competitive production? It doesn't matter if you think "so and so" producer is whack. What matters more is whether or not someone else will like *your* production. In other words, of the producers that you respect and admire, how would honestly rate your production? If you feel that your production can hold its own, then be willing to come down off your price substantially! Let's say in fact, your production does rival some of the best. In the beginning, until you build some notoriety, you will not get paid like some of the best. So proceed with humility, and keep in mind: if the situation presents itself, at least you can aim for a high minimum!

Notes

2. *The overall quality of the Artist and/or persons interested in your beats and music.*

How do you feel about the Artist for whom your beats and music will be used. Be real, if you think that they're very talented, then be prepared to come off your price. If you think that they are extremely talented, and I'm talking like on a level with most critically acclaimed MCs or singers, then be prepared to let go of your beat(s) for nothin', word up. The thing is, if they are what you say, then you should do everything possible to make sure that your production played a part in such a phenomenon. The upside to a situation like this is tremendous. For one thing, you can simply *defer* all payment until some agreed upon future date. This date can be months, even years after the commencement of the project. More importantly, you can secure future production work with this Artist. Work that will undoubtedly garner you even more production work in the future!

On the other hand, if you think that the Artist is really not talented at all, I would first suggest that you reconsider doing production work for them. NEVER WASTE YOUR BEATS on Artists, who neither keep pace with or enhance your production. Going this course once or twice, is o.k., you'll be able to recover. But if you repeatedly go down this road, you will drain yourself of creativity, and in some cases, the drive to even produce. Remember, quality Artists regularly help point producers into more creative more advanced musical directions. Untalented artists often do not understand and/or appreciate your efforts, skill, nor dedication. So a lot of the times, they can have a reverse developmental effect on producers!

3. *Whether or not you will actually get the opportunity to work the session (do the initial tracking, assist the Artist, etc.)*

In some situations, producers sell their beats and do not hear from the Artist/Company for months, even up to a year or so. If you know before hand that you will not be participating in at least the initial recording of the song, then charge towards the mid to high end of the standard price range. If you know before hand that you will be very much involved in the shaping of the song, then stand firm around the mid-price range. The point is to establish what you think your beats and production services are worth, then go about proving it with thorough session management.

Notes

4. *The situation of the Artist and/or persons interested in your beats and music. This can be divided into 4 parts:*
   a. *Is the Artist signed or unsigned?*
   b. *If the Artist is signed, are they signed to a Major Record Label or an Independent Record Label?*
   c. *The size of the Artists Recording Budget.*
   d. *Your gut feeling about the artists potential.*

If the Artist is signed to a Major Record label, proceed with caution. DO NOT ACT LIKE you've never seen a celebrity before! It's O.K. to feel good about your accomplishment, but never appear over excited, or too indebted to the point that you're just happy to be at the session. If your beats and music get you there, represent that to the fullest. Do not forfeit your integrity for anyone. Even though, in certain situations, it may be in your best interest to forgo payment, make it clear that you are doing so of your own free will, not because someone shrewdly duped you out of payday.

If the Artist is signed to an Independent Record label you might have a better chance of getting cash up front, if that's what you're really after. Independents operate on smaller budgets and stricter time constraints, so they like to handle as much as possible for as little as possible. Hence, they use cash as some sort of equalizer. Major Record labels also use cash as an equalizer, but on a much grander scale and usually only among a select group of people. On the other hand, Independents relate well to producers, so they often like to negotiate cash and pay on the spot. In most cases, because they *are* paying cash, (a lot of the time 100% up front), they will get you to come down off your price. So don't feel like you were duped if this happens.

If the Artist is unsigned and *really* talented, try to sign them yourself and offer your production services for free! There are a lot of just O.K. artists these days. In my opinion, there are far too many so-called "hot" Artists that are benefiting from a rather weak talent pool. So if a quality artists approaches you about your production services, do ALL that you can to formulate an alliance. After all, two quality music professions is way more powerful than one!

c. *The size of the Artist's Recording Budget.*

If you know the Artist's budget, you still have to be careful when negotiating price. Again, if the Artist is of high caliber, the most important thing is the production work, not the money… production work will come. So instead

Notes

_____

_____

_____

_____

_____

_____

_____

_____

_____

_____

_____

_____

_____

_____

_____

of seeing how much of the budget you can get, maybe offer multiple beats for the price of one. If the Artist has a sizeable budget, and you know this for certain, as long as your asking price is reasonable, you'll get it. In a case like this, you wanna' be firm with your price... But remember, every price is negotiable!

d. Your gut feeling about the Artist's potential.

Finally, how do you feel about the Artist? I mean, aside from gettin' paid, is the whole project *really* going to be worth your time and production services? There are many cases of talented, but obnoxious Artists, who have a penchant for making sessions, long and nearly disastrous. If you get the feeling that an Artist and or a pro

4. Your personal financial situation

Obviously, your personal financial situation will play some part in whatever price you decide to charge someone for your beats and production services. However, if your financial situation is strenuous, be careful NOT to reveal it. As I mentioned earlier, keep your integrity at all times. Not only will your beat prices be more respected, but you will also be rewarded with more production work. And on the other hand, if you're doing all right financially, do not overemphasize price. The main thing to do is to emphasize additional production opportunities!

All in all, stretch your price range for your beats and services to between 0 and $7,000. There may arise many situations where it is advantageous to you to defer payment in exchange for other benefits; and there may be a few situations where it could be necessary for you to set a very high asking price. Whatever you do, remember that price is always negotiable. However, the framework that might be good to follow looks like this:

> ### A. Quality Artist signed to a Major Record label.
> Price range: $2,500 to $7,000; or 0 (100% deferred).
> *This price should include at least two beats.*
>
> ### B. Quality Artist signed to an Independent label.
> Price range: $500 to $2,500; or 0 (100% deferred).
>
> ### C. Quality unsigned Artist
> Price range: $100 to $1,500; or 0 (100% deferred).

Notes

Contracts and Agreements

Contracts are the written, legal manifestation of all informal and formal negotiations that comprise an agreement between any number of parties. These negotiations or *terms* include, but are certainly not limited to, payment, obligations, commencement, durations, amounts, etc. **Before you begin any project, always make sure that you have thoroughly read over, agreed with, and signed a contract. DO NOT ever accept a handshake or an *honest word* as its substitution!**

Contracts can be as creative as Hip Hop-Rap Production itself. Even though there are industry wide standards, these standards are regularly altered and manipulated in a fashion that *appears* suitable to all parties involved. Hip Hop-Rap Producers and Artists routinely get *shafted*, or rather, taken advantage of, simply because many of us are unfamiliar with contracts. More importantly, we are unfamiliar with the way in which *unique terms and clauses* resonate within various agreements. Therefore, the end result is often a Producer/Artist entering into an unfair agreement.

The biggest reason that some producers enter into unfair agreements is because they simply do not understand that, in reality, ***there is no such thing as a standard contract***. Sure, I concede that there are standard frameworks from which all Music Recording contracts are drafted. However, understanding how and why these contracts are routinely altered, manipulated, and/or totally remodeled is critical to a producer's bottom line: success and compensation.

Always include incentives in your contracts. In my opinion, if a producer has the skills to even get into a contract situation, then they must have the skills to do it again. Hence, go for tangibles over money. That is, whenever possible, try to cover as many non-recoupable costs as possible. For instance, let's say the contract stipulates that you will get paid $5,000 for one beat, with 50% being paid at the signing and another 50% at the completion of the project. You can accept this *standard* format or you can get creative. For example, you can forfeit meal costs, and local travel costs, and up to 25% of the first payment due you, in exchange for a gear and equipment voucher. See, companies have what I call ***wholesale situations*** with all kinds of retail stores, especially Music Gear & Equipment stores. These situations allow Record Companies to purchase loads of gear, at a fraction of its retail price! And it's not even out-of-pocket money because Record Companies pay for these types of services with P.O.s (Purchase

Notes

Order), up to 45 days after the original purchase. Hence, you can an acquire brand new music production setup (*should you choose*) absolutely free and clean. This makes the label happy because they are not really paying you or the artist. This makes the artist happy because more often than not, they can arrange it so that the value of the voucher is not recoupable from their recording budget.

This same situation also works well when dealing with an independent artist. Most independent artists are cash strapped. Ironically, however, they often have O.K. to good credit and other resources. If you make a substantial amount of forfeitures, like the ones already discussed, you could gain anything from gear & equipment to additional royalties.

That being said, examine the following three contracts. Notice their similarities, but also notice the wording of each agreement, and the order of the terms. Also, notice how each agreement is fashioned and shaped in a way that is more suitable for the producer.

Notes

PRODUCTION FOR HIRE AGREEMENT 1

This agreement made on ____/_____/_____(date) is between the Producer and the Undersigned Artist. The Artist has either signed a recording contract with the following Record Company:
_____RECORDS and the date of the contract was ____/_____/_____(date), or is an unsigned/ independent artist.

TERMS AND RECITALS

The effectiveness of this Agreement shall commence with its execution by all of the parties. Please note the following:

a. The Producer specializes in recording, and musical production of musical artists, background recordings, music drops, etc.

b. The Producer is familiar with the musical abilities of Artist.

c. The Artist performs under the name_____ *(if no other name, leave blank)*.

d. The Producer and the Artist wish to enter into this agreement to complete the music production of the songs recorded.

1. PAYMENT

1.1 The Artist/Company, *(whichever applies)*, promises to pay the Producer the following payments in the amount of $_____ per beat *(track or song can be inserted here if you prefer)*. The Artist promises to make payments to the Producer before the pre-production recording phase ___% *(usually 50%, but negotiable)* and as soon as all production is final and approved ___% *(usually remaining balance, but always negotiable. For instance, you can defer payment for other incentives, such as guaranteed future production work)*.

This agreement hereby requests, instructs, authorizes, and empowers the Artist/ Company to pay the Producer all amounts agreed upon. The duration of this agreement commences as of ____/_____/_____(date).

2. PRODUCTION

2.1 The Producer agrees to produce masters of recordings consisting of songs performed by Artist (hereinafter referred to as the "Songs"). The resulting

Notes

recording (hereinafter referred to as the "Recording") shall be of a quality that is equal to master recordings normally produced for commercial distribution. The Artist will also give production credits (full or Co) to the Producer(s) in both written and verbal formats. (I.E. Album credits, or person-to-person inquiries).

3. CONTRIBUTION BY ARTIST

3.1 The Artist agrees to fully cooperate with the Producer, in good faith, in the production of the Recording; to contribute to such production the music and lyrics embodied in the Songs; to arrange, direct and perform the Songs in such a manner as to facilitate the production of the Recording; and to otherwise strictly observe the remaining duties and obligations of this Agreement.

4. ARTISTIC CONTROL

4.1 The Producer and the Artist shall be jointly responsible for all decisions regarding the artistic content of the Recording. The Producer shall maintain final decision rights in the event mutual consensus is not reached.

5. TITLE

5.1 The title of the Recording shall be chosen by agreement between the Producer and the Artist.

6. DATES AND LOCATION OF RECORDING SESSIONS

6.1 The recording sessions necessary to produce the Recordings will occur at studios and facilities chosen by the Producer.

7. ADDITIONAL MUSICIANS

7.1 The _____ (Artist) or _____ (Producer) shall provide and compensate sufficient and competent musicians to properly perform the Songs, as arranged and directed by the Artist and the Producer.

8. COSTS

8.1 The Producer and the Artist will be responsible for deciding in advance who will pay all of the costs that will be incurred in the production of the

Notes

Recording, including the prepayment of all travel, hotel and meal costs incurred by the Artist and/ or the Producer in attending the recording sessions .

9. COMPLETION AND RELEASE

9.1 If the Artist or the Company plans to release and distribute the Recording(s), the Recording(s) shall be completed and prepared for release and distribution on or before ____/_____/_____ (date). The Artist or the Artist's Company will be responsible for the release and distribution of the Recordings. If the Artist or the Artist's Company isn't ready to release and distribute the Recording(s) by the date previously aforementioned, the Artist will notify the Producer and will continue to give frequent updates concerning the status of the recordings. The Artist will also inform the Producer once the final release and distribution dates are determined. The Producer and the Artist acknowledge that time is of the essence in the completion of the Recording, and they each agree to exercise all reasonable means to achieve such completion.

10. COPYRIGHT

10.1 Upon the Artist's assignment of the Songs pursuant herein, the _____ (Producer) or (Artist) or (Company), whichever applies, shall proceed to obtain and secure a copyright for each of the said Songs. Each such copyright shall be the sole property of both the Producer *(designate your publishing company, i.e. ASCAP, BMI)* and the Artist/company, *(whichever applies)*, 50/50.

11. SAMPLE CLEARANCE

11.1 The Artist understands that the Producer may have utilized a sample from another artist's (s) recording, which was previously copyrighted, to create the beat (music, track, song, etc.). The Producer will give the Artist full disclosure of the origin of all samples. In the event that the song from the recording is published, utilizing the beat (music, track) the Artist/company, *(whichever applies)*, will assume all responsibility for clearing any samples utilized. In the event that there's a lawsuit, the Artist/company, *(whichever applies)*, and NOT the Producer, will assume all responsibility for settling the copyright infringement and the Producer will not be liable. If the name of an artist sampled for the beat (music, track, etc.) is required, the Artist will consult the Producer and will get the information concerning the origin of the sample(s) utilized in the song. In the event that the Artist is not able to retrieve the name of a sampled artist(s) from the Producer, the Artist will be responsible in obtaining the names of any sampled

Notes

artist(s) and getting the sample(s) cleared. The Artist/Company, *(whichever applies)* will accept total responsibility and liability for any changes made to the tracks after the Producer's has delivered the master track(s).

13. UNDERSTANDING

13.1 The Artist/Company, *(whichever applies)* and the Producer understand that this written agreement is a legally binding document. In the event that either the Artist/Company, *(whichever applies)* or the Producer violates any of the above clauses, each understands that they will be liable for damages and attorney fees.

By signing their signatures below or executing the purchase online, both the Artist and the Producer agree with all the terms and conditions written in this written agreement.

Print: X_____   Date_____/_____/_____

Sign: X_____   Artist/Company, *(whichever applies)*

Print: X_____   Date_____/_____/_____

Sign: X_____   Witness

Print: X_____   Date_____/_____/_____

Sign: X_____   Producer

Print: X_____   Date_____/_____/_____

Sign: X_____   Witness

Notes

PRODUCTION FOR HIRE AGREEMENT 2

This is a Production Agreement this day of ____, 200_, between the Master Producer (You/Your Production Company) _____ and the Undersigned Artist_____. The Artist has signed a recording contract with the following Company _____, and the date of the contract was _____ 200_, or the Artist is unsigned and/or independent. All references to the Master Producer, Producer, "Us", "We", and/or "I", and the like will hereby refer to the aforementioned Master Producer and/or Producer employed by the Master Producer, only. All references to the Artist/Company, and/or "You" and the like will hereby refer to the aforementioned Artist/Company, only.

1. SERVICES AND OBLIGATIONS

1.1 In this Production Agreement, the Master Producer is a work for hire for only ___ recording(s).

1.2 PRODUCTION

1.2.(a) The Producer agrees to produce masters of recordings consisting of songs performed by Artist (hereinafter referred to as the "Songs"). The resulting recording (hereinafter referred to as the "Recording") shall be of a quality that is equal to master recordings normally produced for commercial distribution. The Artist will also give production credits (full or Co) to the Producer(s) in both written and verbal formats. (I.E. Album credits, or person-to-person inquiries).

1.3. ARTIST CONTRIBUTION

1.3.(b) The Artist agrees to fully cooperate with the Producer, in good faith, in the production of the Recording; to contribute to such production the music and lyrics embodied in the Songs; to arrange, direct and perform the Songs in such a manner as to facilitate the production of the Recording; and to otherwise strictly observe the remaining duties and obligations of this Agreement. The Artist shall be responsible for booking all associated recording sessions, and shall be responsible for notifying the Master Producer/Producer at least ___ hours prior to the commencement of any recording sessions.

Notes

3. PAYMENT

3.1 Artist/Company, *(whichever applies)*, promises to pay Master Producer/Production Company the following payments in the amount of $_____ per beat *(track or song can be inserted here if you prefer)*. The Artist/Company, *(whichever applies)*, promises to make payments to the Producer before the pre-production recording phase ___% *(usually 50%, but negotiable)* and as soon as all production is final and approved ___% *(usually remaining balance, but always negotiable. For instance, you can defer payment for other incentives, such as guaranteed future production work)*.

3.1.(a) This Production Agreement hereby requests, instructs, authorizes, and empowers Record Company(in your case the artist) to pay Master Producer(or production company) all producer fees agreed upon.

4. COSTS

4.1 The Artist/Company, *(whichever applies)*, will be responsible for paying all of the costs that will be incurred in the production of the Recording, including the prepayment of all travel, hotel and meal costs incurred by the Producer in attending the recording sessions . Costs that are NOT prepaid shall be recoupable by the Producer within ___ business days, from the time the Artist/Company receives receipts of such legitimate costs.

5. Miscellaneous

5.1 This Production Agreement can and will be used in a court of law (city, state) in the event that there is a breach of these contractual provisions.

6. COPYRIGHT

6.1 By signing this Agreement you (Artist) hereby grant our publishing designee 50% of your share of world-wide copyrights for this recording.

The duration of this agreement commences as of the date of the contact between the Artist and the Master Producer(Production Company) ____ ,200_.

Notes

By signing their signatures below or executing the purchase online, both the Artist and the Producer agree with all the terms and conditions written in this written agreement.

Print: X_____   Date____/____/____

Sign: X_____   Artist/Company, *(whichever applies)*

Print: X_____   Date____/____/____

Sign: X_____   Witness

Print: X_____   Date____/____/____

Sign: X_____ Producer

Print: X_____Date____/____/____

Sign: X_____ Witness

Master Producer: (You) _____

Notes

EXCLUSIVE PRODUCTION AGREEMENT
(Used for the purpose of signing other producers to your Production Company)

This is a Production Agreement, (hereinafter referred to as the "Agreement") this day of _____ 200_, between the Master Producer, ("You", producing under the pseudonym, "_____") and the Production Company, ("Us"). Hereinafter the company shall be referred to as "the Production Company" and/or the "Company" and/or "Us".

1. SERVICES/TERMS

1.1 The term will commence on the date hereof and will continue, unless extended as provided herein, for ___ years.

1.2 During the term of the Agreement, you will render your personal production services exclusively to us, as the producer of Pre-Mastered Recordings, hereby referred to as "Beats". The company has the Full and Exclusive right to negotiate price and payment for all of your beats and production services.

1.2.(a) Your beats shall be produced and used for any one and/or combination of the following:

1.2.(a1) For the purpose of creating songs, backgrounds, interludes, intros, outros, and the like for all of the Company's recording artists and producers.

1.2.(a2) For the purpose of creating songs, backgrounds, interludes, intros, outros, and the like for any artist(s) and/or other like person(s) NOT signed to the Company.

1.2.(a3) The producer agrees to give the Company the Full and Exclusive right to stipulate and negotiate any and all terms of agreements associated with your beats produced for any artist(s) and/or other like person(s) NOT signed to the company. This DOES NOT mean that the company is, nor shall ever be, the producer's manager. The producer shall have the right to enter into a Management Agreement with whom they choose. However, it is understood that all terms of this agreement shall remain intact, throughout the term specified in section 1, sub-section 1.1.

Notes

1.3 Your production role in the studio:

1.3.(a) In regards to the beats that you produce for _____ and other Company artists, it shall be no less than your assistance with the tracking of your beats. That is, you are required to be present at the recording session, whenever the initial tracking of your beats are being performed, unless otherwise noted in writing by us. ALL final mixes and/or master recordings of your beats and/or songs is the sole responsibility of the Company.

1.3.(b) In regards to the beats that you produce for anyone NOT signed to the Company, you shall be required to perform or assist in performing the initial tracking of your beats.

1.4 In the event that you can not be present for an initial tracking recording session, you must give us at least 3 days notice. You must also deliver any beat in consideration for any Company related project, within 48hrs of said notice.

1.4.(a) The following formats of beats shall be deemed suitable for delivery to us:

1.4.(a1) 2 inch reel to reel.

1.4.(a2) Pro Tools data CD, with two additional backups.

1.4.(b) The time length of each beat that shall be deemed suitable for delivery to us:

1.4.(b1) 5 minutes or more, but not too exceed 8 minutes, unless otherwise expressed by us in writing.

2. PRODUCTION CREDITS AND RECOGNITION

2.1 For beats produced for any recording artist signed to the Company: You will receive Full Production credit, in regards to any and all beats that you produce. Production credit for the song (single or album) shall read like this, "Produced by "You" for the Company (Us).

2.3 For beats produced for artists NOT signed to the Company, you will receive Full Production credit.

Notes

_____

_____

_____

_____

_____

_____

_____

_____

_____

_____

_____

_____

3. OBLIGATIONS

3.1 Producer Obligations:

3.1.(a)You are obligated to submit at least 3 brand new beats to us every week.

3.1.(b) You are obligated to perform such services as are customarily performed by a record producer, including but not limited to, editing/sequencing, tracking, and the initial recording of your beats.

3.1.(c) You are obligated to produce and perform under the alias, "_____" and/or "_____".

3.1.(d) You are obligated to report any and all inquiries about your production services to the Company.

The "Key Man"[1] in this clause is _____.

3.1.(e) You are obligated to assist in the promotion and marketing of your production services.

3.2 Company Obligations

3.2.(a) The Company is obligated to identify, seek, find, and foster artists for your production services. These artists shall be of a talent level approved by both the Producer and the Company. Though the Company has final say over which artists the Producer can produce for, the company must inform the Producer of any and all inquiries, in regards to the Producer's beats and production services.

3.2.(b) The Company is obligated to promote and market your beats and production services, worldwide, via customary promotional practices and channels, including but not limited to, industry contacts, online promotional campaigns, business cards, flyers, etc.

---

[1] The "Key Man" is the contact person. Key Man clauses are very important. People routinely move around in the Music Recording Business. Pressures run extremely high, which often translates into a strange culture of impulsive promotions and terminations. Because so many people are fired, hired and/or relocated, the changes essentially jeopardize the situations of everyone directly associated. *Key Man clauses* makes it clear which Company Representative will be dealing direct (the majority of the time) with the Producer/Artist. Key Man clauses also give Producers/Artists a way out of an agreement, in the event that the Key Man (contact person) departs from the Company.

Notes

3.2.(c) The Company is obligated to negotiate and secure price and payment for your beats and production services with any artist and like persons NOT signed to the company.

3.2.(c) With regards to artists and the like NOT signed to the Company, the Company is obligated to secure a purchasing price for your beats and production services that is NO LESS THAN $_____ per beat. After _ months from the date of this agreement, this minimum amount shall increase to NO LESS THAN $_____ per beat produced by you.

3.3   The Company is obligated to secure production work for you NO LESS THAN once per month. In the event that the Company does not secure production work for you, whether it be for any artist signed to the Company or any artist and the like NOT signed to the Company, within any given 6-month period, the Company must pay you an non-recoupable fee of $_____, within 7 days of the ending of that month. If the Company DOES NOT secure any production work for you at any time, within ANY 6 month period, the Company must pay you a non-recoupable fee of $_____, within 30 days of the ending of that 6 month period. However, within this 30-day period, if the Company secures production work for you, the $_____ payment shall be considered null and void.

4. ROYALTIES

4.1 On songs made for the Company:

As full consideration for all of the rights granted to the Company hereunder and provided you have fully complied with all of your material obligations, hereunder, the Company will pay you, subject to all the terms and conditions hereof, a royalty computed at the applicable percentage indicated below of the applicable Royalty Base Price with respect to the Net Sale of Records consisting entirely of Recordings recorded hereunder and sold by the company or its licensees through Normal Retail Channels in the United States ("UNRC Net Sales"), for a period of 5 years. Such royalties shall be inclusive of all royalties payable to you of the Recordings made hereunder:

4.1.(a) On Records, Compact Discs and/or Cassette Tapes, (in which at least one of your beats have been used in the creation of at least one of the songs) sold for distribution in the United States:

Notes

4.1.(a1) On Albums: _% (_ royalty per unit)[2]

4.1.(a2) On Singles: _% _ royalty per unit)

4.1.(a3) The royalty rates pursuant to subsection 4.1(a)(1) will apply to the first five hundred (500,000) units of UNRC Net Sales in the United States ("USNRC Net Sales") of each Album consisting of Master Recordings made hereunder. The applicable royalty rates will be increased by _% on the next five hundred units of USNRC Net Sales of any such Album, and by another _% on USNRC Net Sales of any such Album in excess of 1 million (1,000,000) units.

4.1.(b) On Records, Compact Discs and/or Cassette Tapes Sold for Distribution Outside The United States:

4.1.(b.1) __% (__) on Albums and/or Singles sold for distribution in Canada.

4.1.(b.2) __% (__) on albums and/or Singles sold for distribution in Japan, The U.K., France, Germany, Italy, Spain, Belgium, and the Netherlands; and

4.1.(b.3) __% (__) on albums and/or Singles sold for distribution elsewhere.

4.2. The Company shall not pay you any royalty On Audiovisual Recordings, such as videos, films or television shows and commercials.

5. PAYMENT PER BEAT

As full consideration for all of the rights granted to the Company hereunder and provided you have fully complied with all of your material obligations, hereunder, the Company will pay you, subject to all the terms and conditions hereof, a payment sum of:

5.1 On your beats used for any artist signed to the Company:

5.1.(a) Not less than $_____, no more than $_____ for any number of beats up to 3. Whichever amount is at the sole discretion of the Company.

5.1.(b) Not less than $_____, no more than $_____ for any number of beats between 4 and 6. Whichever amount is at the sole discretion of the Company.

---

[2] Please see Royalty Rate Computation.

Notes

5.1. (c) With regards to beats used by any artist signed to the Company, the Company will pay _% of the payment up front, at the commencement of the initial tracking session. The Company shall pay the remaining _% of the payment to you within two weeks of the completion of the final mix of the song(s), in which your beat(s) was (were) used.

5.2 On your beats used for artists NOT signed by the Company, in particular, artists and the like whom the Company has secured and entered in with a agreement for your production services:

5.2.(a) _% of the purchasing price paid for your production.
Please note. _% of the purchasing price shall be retained by the Company, as its percentage.

5.4 With regards to beats purchase from artists and the like NOT signed to the Company, All payments owed to you shall be paid to you within two weeks of the Company's receipt of such applicable payments.

6 EXPENSES

6.1 With regards to Costs incurred in the Production of the Recording:

6.1.(a) As full consideration for all of the rights granted to the company hereunder and provided you have fully complied with all of your material obligations, hereunder, the Company will pre-pay for all of your costs incurred in the production of recordings for artists signed to the Company, and artists NOT signed the Company—provided they have entered into an agreement with the Company for your beats and production services, and have agreed to pre-pay us for your costs incurred, during the use of your production services.

7. ACCOUNTINGS

7.1. The Company will render statements on October 31 and April 30 of each year of all royalties due and owing to you at the end of the semi-annual periods ending on the preceding June 30 and December 31, respectively. Such statements shall be accompanied by payment of royalties shown to be due and owed to you, if any, after deducting any and all un-recouped Advances and chargeable costs under this agreement.

7.2. We will maintain books and records which report the sales of the Phonograph Records, Compact Discs and/or Cassette Tapes. You may, at your own expense,

Notes

examine those books and records, as provided in this paragraph only. You may make those examinations only for the purpose of verifying the accuracy of the statements sent to you under paragraph 4.1. You may make such an examination for a particular statement only once, and only within two (2) years after the date when we send you that statement under paragraph 4.1. (We will be deemed conclusively to have sent you each statement on the date prescribed in 4.1 unless you notify us otherwise, with respect to any statement, within thirty (30) days after that date.) You may make those examinations only during our usual business hours, and at the place where we keep the books and records to be examined. If you wish to make an examination you will be required to notify us at least thirty (30) days before the date when you plan to begin it. We may postpone commencement of your examination by notice given to you no later than five (5) business days before the commencement date specified in your notice; if we do so, the running of the time within which the examination may be made will be suspended during the postponement. If your examination has not been completed within one month from the time you begin it, we may require you to terminate it on seven (7) business days' notice to you at any time; we will not be required to permit you to continue the examination after the end of that seven-day period.

7.3 If you have any objections to a royalty statement, you will give us specific notice of that objection and your reasons for it within two (2) years after the date when we send you that statement under paragraph 7.1.

8. MISCELLANEOUS.

8.1. Neither party will be entitled to recover damages or to terminate this agreement by reason of any breach hereof by the other party, that otherwise entitle you to recover damages or the right to terminate this agreement, unless the latter party has failed to substantially remedy such breach within a reasonable time following receipt of your notice thereof. For the purposes of this paragraph 8.1 and solely with respect to our obligation to make payments to you under this agreement, "reasonable time" shall be forty-five (45) days, it being understood however, that you shall not be entitled to recover damages or terminate the term of this agreement if the breach of our payment obligation cannot be remedied within thirty (30) days, and we have commenced to remedy it within that time and have proceeded with reasonable promptness.

Notes

8.2: YOU WILL BE CONSIDERED IN BREACH IF YOU:

8.2.(a) Negotiate ANY production agreement with any Artist and the like signed or not signed to the Company, without the expressed, written consent of the Company.

8.2.(b) Provide ANY of your beats and/or production services to any artist and the like, for any project, whether it be for free or payment, without the expressed, written consent of the Company.

8.3. TERMINATION

8.3.(a) This agreement may be terminated by the Company at any time, for ANY reason. The Company's desire to terminate the agreement must be presented to you in writing. However, any and all monies remaining due to you must be paid to you within forty-five (45) days of the termination of the agreement. If you do not receive monies owed to you within forty-five (45) days of the termination of the agreement, the agreement is automatically reinstated.

8.3.(b) You may remove yourself from this contract at any time with a one-time buy-out fee of $_____. If you buy out of the agreement with the Company, any and all royalties owed to shall be forfeited, immediately.

8.4. This agreement contains the entire understanding of the parties. No change of this agreement will be binding upon us unless it is made by an instrument duly executed by us. No change of this agreement will be binding on you unless it is made by an instrument signed by you.

8.5. This agreement will be governed and construed pursuant to the laws of the State of _____ applicable to contracts entered into and performed entirely within the State of _____, and any disputes or controversies arising hereunder shall be subject to the jurisdiction of Courts of the State of _____ or of the U.S. Federal District Court for the _____ District of _____. Any process in any action or proceeding arising under or relating to this agreement may, among other methods, be served upon you by delivering or mailing the same by registered or certified mail, directed to the address first written above or such other address as you designate by notice to us. Any such delivery or mail service shall be deemed to have the same force and effect as personal service within the State of _____.

Notes

8.6. All notices hereunder shall be in writing and shall be given by personal delivery, registered or certified mail, return receipt requested, or by Federal Express, at the addresses shown above, or such other address or addresses as may from time to time be designated by either party by notice. Notices shall be deemed to be given when mailed, except for a notice of change of address which shall be deemed to be given on the date of its receipt.

8.7. You may not assign this agreement or any of your rights hereunder to anyone.

8.8. In entering into this agreement, and in providing your services pursuant hereto, you have and shall have the status of an independent contractor and nothing herein contained shall contemplate or constitute you as our agent or employee. Should you become an agent or employee of us, your second year salary will be comparable to the salary of your current highest executive position—no less than $_____ annually, and no more than $_____ annually. An agent/employee agreement, prepared by us and approved by you, must be signed by both parties, prior to you becoming an agent or employee of us.

8.9. This agreement shall not become effective until executed by all proposed parties hereto.

8.10 You have read and fully understand this agreement. You have either consulted with an attorney regarding any questions you may have or have voluntarily elected not to do so.

Notes

IN WITNESS WHEREOF, the parties have executed this agreement on the date and year first written above.

Witness_____

By_____   _____
   Officer,   Producer
   The Company ,

My social security number is_____. Under the penalties of perjury, I certify that this information is true, correct and complete.

YOUR ASSENT AND GUARANTY.

To induce the Company to enter into the forgoing agreement with the Producer, "_____", "_____", (the "Agreement"):

1. _____ (Producer)

1.(a) represents to us that he has read the Agreement and has had the legal effect of each of its provisions of it relating to the Producer, and the Company, and artists NOT SIGNED to the Company.

1.(c) acknowledges that we will have no obligation to make any payments to the Producer in connection with the services rendered by the Producer or the fulfillment of the Producer other obligations under the Agreement, except for the payments specified in paragraphs 4, 5, and 6.

Notes

2.(a) "_____" (The Producer):

2.(a.1) agrees to indemnify and hold us harmless from any loss, damage, liability or expense (including but not limited to attorney's fees and legal expenses) which arise from any failure by us to fulfill our obligations under the agreement.

_____

Producer

ROYALTY RATE COMPUTATION

$9.98	Average retail price of cassettes
-1.45	15% Packaging deduction
$8.53	
-1.99	10% of $9.98 deduction for free goods
$7.54	Amount Producer's royalties are really based on
$7.54	Amount Producer's royalties are really based on
X. %	Producer's royalty rate
_____	Producer's royalty per unit

Notes

AFTER WORD

THE MAIN REASON THAT SO many Hip Hop-Rap producers ultimately stop and give it up is because they never develop their own production identity. There are a number of factors that contribute to this. However, I believe that this phenomenon is mainly attributed to three factors: 1. The lack of thorough practice; 2. The lack of a concrete understanding and appreciation and/or respect for Music History; and 3. The fact that most producers never really learn HOW to "use" their gear in the "best" (not most popular) manner. I designed BeatTips™ to address these factors. In fact, my overriding goal is to directly offer the most critical, comprehensive (**widely unknown**) information on making Hip Hop-Rap Beats and Music; while at the same time, provide insight on the entire process that both underscores and surrounds it. I am primarily concerned with getting this information to producers (and/or those persons interested in becoming producers), who might not otherwise be able to receive it.

The current shameless duplication of unimaginative, unchallenging, low-quality Hip Hop-Rap Music Production is one of the most unfortunate trends in the history of Hip Hop-Rap. It has been my central aim to help producers defeat this awful trend, by stressing one theme: that **"quality production is directly linked to the development of a producer's own unique sound and style."** To this end, I have attempted to explain and share some of the most critical production tips that I have created, discovered and learned. My only hope is that this attempt contributes to the resurgence of more original, sincere, quality-based Hip Hop-Rap Music.

I would also like to tell all producers to be real about what your aim is. Mastering the craft of Hip Hop-Rap Beats and Music is uniquely difficult and ongoing. No matter what gear you have or how you use it, you will not advance if you're not clear and honest about what your aim is. If your aim is to make beats and music somewhere in the tradition of how this culture emerged, then pursue it with the zeal of a future musical pioneer. But realize, though admirable as that might be, it is not in line with the current "commercial Gangster Pop and Club-Thug sound". So make sure that you identify and pursue your market wisely.

On the other hand, If your aim is simply to duplicate the current sound of today, in an effort to gain big money—which I completely understand, but do not recommend— then be advised: it is not likely that your production skills will ever properly advance. In fact, if you focus on the wholesale biting of this current "club-thug" style of Hip Hop-Rap music, you will actually make it more difficult to earn a living from your production services. Keep in mind, there is a large number of contemporary producers (both well-known and unknown), who are perfectly comfortable with the idea of simply, "copying" the dominant trend of the times. Indeed, a producer *should* be able to deliver the sound of the times. But I also believe that those producers who can develop and balance their own unique sound, while at the same time satisfy current music trends, are in a better position to receive both production work and critical acclaim.

Notes

Here, I must point out that I don't knock *anyone* for how they produce, or what they use to produce, for that matter. I understand and respect the relevance of current themes and current sound-trends. Hip Hop-Rap has been in the midst of a sound-trend for the past 7 years… Call it Popular; call it "Commercial", call it "Video Gangster"; call it "Pink Production"; call it "Club-Thug", whatever—the current Hip Hop–Rap music scene (whack, unoriginal, or not) appeals to a great number of producers, for various reasons. The most noticeable reason is that it offers the fastest route to getting paid! Now, the lone prospect of simply *getting paid* doesn't necessarily appeal to me. But as a producer, I have to respect the fact that it appeals to many others. This generic "mass appeal production", so to speak, is perhaps one of the biggest reasons that the overall quality and creativity in Hip Hop-Rap production has suffered over the last 7 years. Some time, not too long ago, I don't know exactly when, it became acceptable, and in some cases, cool, to bite and aggressively copy the sound of other producers and/or rappers! During this same time, it also became O.K. for producers to just do the bare minimum. Whether or not any of the established producers and pioneers spoke up against this trend isn't important. Neither is a discussion about the influence of the Major Recording Labels and the various media outlets that "control" Hip Hop-Rap circulation. **The important thing to always remember is that: producers, for better OR worse, *always* dictate the current sound of the times.**

Finally, consider this fact: Hip Hop-Rap, and music in general, shifts continuously. At times, this shift is more profound and obvious. Well, the shift in Hip Hop-Rap (albeit subtly), has begun. The number of musically sophisticated fans, who lack the tolerance for unchallenging and uninspiring music, is growing. This has been loudly exemplified in the substantial decreases in retail sales (of music) over the past 5 years, and counting…

Even though these factors may seem to point to the demise of quality Hip Hop-Rap, I do believe that the term "popular music" will soon once again come to define music that is based on good songwriting, inspiring rhythms and pioneering production! Also, remember this: there are a handful of well-known M.C.s, who are really making serious efforts to raise the level of their lyrical content. But even more profound than that is the fact that there are a countless number of emerging "unknown" M.C.s, who are rejecting the popular "fluff and floss" formula of contemporary Hip Hop-Rap Music. These *new* M.C.s are only looking for the kinds of beats and music that can accompany and inspire their developing styles. So, for all you Hip Hop-Rap Music producers, who are preparing and customizing your sounds, styles and techniques, in expectation of this new, more relevant breed of M.C.s, keep creatin'…you will ultimately find yourselves in an excellent position.

One…
Sa'id

APPENDIX
Performance Rights Societies

American Society of Composers, Authors and Publishers (ASCAP)

New York

One Lincoln Plaza
New York, NY 10023
(212) 621-6000

Los Angeles

7920 Sunset Blvd., Suite 300
Los Angeles, CA 90046
(213) 883-1000

Nashville

2 Music Square West
Nashville, TN 37203
(615) 742-5000

Broadcast Music, Inc. (BMI)

New York

320 W. 57th St.
New York, NY 10019
(212) 586-2000

Los Angeles

8730 Sunset Blvd., 3rd Floor West
Los Angeles, CA 90069
(310) 659-9109

Nashville

10 Music Square East
Nashville, TN 37203
(615) 401-2000

SESAC

New York

421 W. 54th St.
New York, NY 10019
(212) 586-3450

Nashville

55 Music Square East
Nashville, TN 37203
(615) 320-0055

Sites and Production Related Services

Online Used and New Gear & Equipment Online Stores
www.daddys.com
(Daddy's Junky Music… if they don't have it, they can get it!)
www.8thstreet.com
www.djsupply.com
www.gand.com
www.melmusic.com (They're in Australia, but they ALWAYS have rare gear.)
www.melodyexchange.com
www.grandmas.com
www.ebay.com
www.twolinesmusic.com
(They're in New York City. I've done business with them for years.)

Websites for Drums, Memory Expansion Cards, Backlights, etc.
www.soundcrafting.com
www.hiphopdrums.com
www.masterbits.com
www.primesounds.com
www.telesisgear.com

Gear & Equipment Information & Reference Websites
www.sonicstate.com (Great information, massive links.)
www.emusician.com
www.onestopbeats.com/beattalk
www.millimeter.com
www.synthmuseum.com
www.wired.com

Music and Production Related Services
www.totalsonicmedia.com (CD & Vinyl Mastering, Duplication, large or small runs, Best prices, *fast turn around*. The owner will work with your situation.)
Docufit™ Graphics (718) 981-0861, (contact: Sharon, service is excellent; prices are unbeatable!)
Marlo Copying and Printing (212) 967-1290, (contact: Jayson or Leo)
www.stopnprint.com (Flyers, Posters, etc.)
www.creativemoonlighter.com (Organization of freelance photographers, web designers, graphic designers, etc. They actually bid on your project.)

Websites/Online Forums of Interest for Producers/Artists
www.superchampnyc.com (This is the website for Superchamp Records.)
www.45king.com
www.gangstaronline.com
www.rapflava.com
www.futureproducers.com

www.fatbeats.com

www.sandboxautomatic.com
www.allhiphop.com
www.daveyd.com
www.b-boys.com
www.accesshiphop.com
www.rapbattles.com
www.rapboard.com
www.radiomute.com
www.typeill.com
www.rapworlds.com
www.odcproductionz.com (rapture forums)
www.allhiphop.com
www.midiworld.com
www.remixmag.com
www.rapdogs.com
www.synthzone.com
www.telesisgear.com
http://code404.com/synths/index-text.html
www.vintagesynth.org
www.vintagesynth.com

Promotions
www.blankshirts.com
www.cafepress.com
www.ngslater.com

Akai S950/Akai MPC 60II Production Setup Budget

Akai S95O
Excellent working/cosmetic condition, with full memory: **$450**.
(With standard memory: **$250-$350**)

Akai MPC 60II
Excellent working/cosmetic condition (memory expansion not needed if you use Akai MPC 60II only as a sequencer): **$600- $850.**

Mackie 1604 VLZ 16 Channel Mixing Board
Brand new: **$900**
Used, in excellent working/cosmetic condition: **$400-$500.**

Hafler P3000 Amplifier
Brand new: **$900 -$1,100**
Used: **$300-$500**

Technics SB-LX50 Speakers
Brand new: **$150** for the pair.
Used: **$75** for the pair.

Numark DM1200 (DJ) Mixer
Brand new: **$110**

Technics Direct Drive SL-MK2 Turntable
Brand new: **$479**

HHB CDR 850 CD Recorder
Brand new: **$800**

Tascam 302 Cassette Deck
Brand new: **$250**

Panasonic CT 20614A 20" Video Monitor/TV.
Brand new: **$235**

Panasonic PV-9661 VHS
Brand new: **$150**

Note.

If your money is limited and you are only able to purchase each unit, one at a time, follow the order of the preceding list, starting with the Akai S950, followed by the Akai MPC 60II.
Total budget: $3,000 - $4,000.

Also, keep in mind that though this setup is exceptional, in and of itself, you should also consider acquiring a late-model keyboard at some point! The addition of a keyboard will only broaden your musical understanding, especially with regards to arrangements, measures, melodies and the like.

Note about Reference Monitors Vs. Speakers

Any pair of old speakers with good bass, can be used. However, I do not recommend investing in Reference Monitors for a home studio. Reason why: I believe in training your ear to how you *want* your music to sound. Reference Monitors are usually incorporated by engineers during the tracking and mixing phase. And even then some engineers prefer tracking while listening mainly to the "Mids" (Mid Level) Speakers. But if you do decide that you would like to get Reference Monitors, go with the Yamaha NS-10. They are the standard of nearly every professional recording studio.

Index

Diagram of my setup hooked up

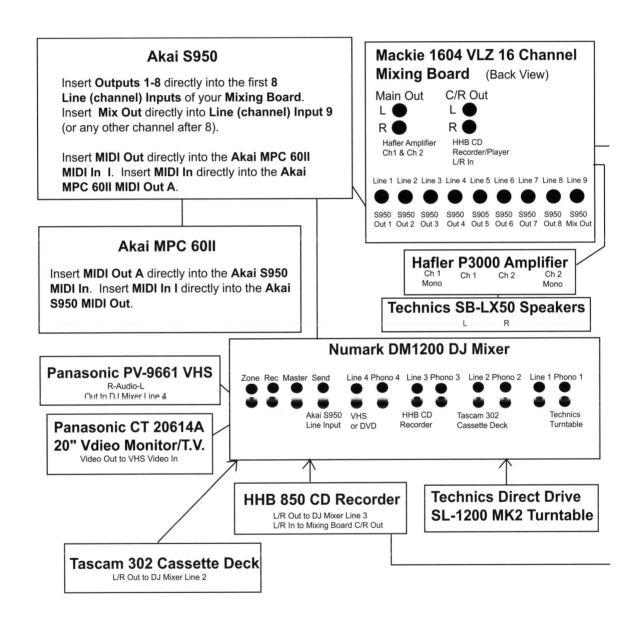

What up.

In a continuing effort to play my part in the development of Hip Hop-Rap Music, Producers and Culture, I have authorized my company, SUPERCHAMP, INC., to issue *two* **$250** *grants*, every month to aspiring Hip Hop-Rap Producers and/or Recording Artists.

These grants can be used to help purchase gear & equipment, records, promotional flyers, studio time, supplies... Or however the grant recipients see fit!

Qualified applicants must show a dedicated interest in their field, as well as some level of skill.

There is no strict age requirement, but applicants should be at least 16 years old.

Finally, a portion of the proceeds from every **BeatTips™ Manual** sold will be used to help fund the **SUPERCHAMP Quality Films and Music Grants™** program.

For more details and to learn how to apply, go to:
www.superchampgrants.com.

one
Sa'id

Need To Order Another
BeatTips™ Manual
Here It Is . . .

Name: _____

Company: _____

Address: _____

Apartment No. _____ City: _____ State: _____

Country: _____ Zip Code: _____ - _____

Email: _____ Phone No. _____

Quantity	
Item	**BeatTips™ Manual**
Price **per book** inside USA + $6.00 Shipping & Handling	**$25.95**
Price **per book** in Canada + $12.00 Shipping & Handling	**$38.95**

International orders Flat Rate Shipping: $40.95 (U.S. Dollars) per book

Please make checks payable to Supercham Inc.	**Amount Enclosed:**

Mail To:

SUPERCHAMP
Books™
A Division of SUPERCHAMP, INC.
930 Cleveland Street, 1st Floor Brooklyn, NY 11208
(718) 272-4202, (917) 270-2005   www.superchampnyc.com

Please allow two weeks for delivery

Visit our website: at : www.superchampbooks.com
Check out SA'ID's new album: Keep It Movin' - Coming Soon